Iliyana Stareva

Social Media and the Rebirth of PR

The Emergence of Social Media as a Change Driver for PR

Anchor Academic Publishing

Stareva, Iliyana: Social Media and the Rebirth of PR: The Emergence of Social Media as a Change Driver for PR. Hamburg, Anchor Academic Publishing 2013

Buch-ISBN: 978-3-95489-178-8
PDF-eBook-ISBN: 978-3-95489-678-3
Druck/Herstellung: Anchor Academic Publishing, Hamburg, 2013

Bibliografische Information der Deutschen Nationalbibliothek:
Die Deutsche Nationalbibliothek verzeichnet diese Publikation in der Deutschen Nationalbibliografie; detaillierte bibliografische Daten sind im Internet über http://dnb.d-nb.de abrufbar.

Bibliographical Information of the German National Library:
The German National Library lists this publication in the German National Bibliography. Detailed bibliographic data can be found at: http://dnb.d-nb.de

Hermannstal 119k, 22119 Hamburg
http://www.diplomica-verlag.de, Hamburg 2013
Printed in Germany

Table of Contents

List of Tables

List of Figures

Acknowledgements

It is a great pleasure to thank everyone who was involved in this research.

Firstly, I would like to show my gratitude to my supervisor, Andrew Morton, who supported me throughout the whole process by not only advising me about what is right and how things should be done, but also by giving me some thoughtful ideas.

I would also like to thank all survey and interview participants for their interest in my study as well as everyone who helped me promote and distribute the questionnaire.

Finally, this research would not have been possible without the constant encouragement of my family and friends. At this point, I would like to express my utmost gratitude to my mom – Teodora Stareva – who showed me how to "lean in".

Iliyana Stareva

Abbreviations

The following commonly accepted abbreviations have been used throughout the report to ensure ease of reading and digestion of the discussed material:

CIPR – *Chartered Institute of Public Relations*[1]

PR – *Public Relations*

PRO – *Public Relations Officer*

PRSA – *Public Relations Society of America*[2]

SM – *Social Media*

UGG – *User-Generated Content*

[1] CIPR is the professional body for PR practitioners in the UK.
[2] PRSA is the world's largest organisation for PR professionals.

1. Introduction

The Public Relations industry has faced dramatic changes in the past few years in terms of new technology and media channels as well as new opportunities for communicating with clients and businesses. The main **reason for this is the emergence of social media networking** which enabled customers to easily and quickly engage in a two-way communication process with companies. For businesses on the other hand this represents a **huge challenge of how to effectively handle the new forms of engagement** so that they now realize the increasing importance of public relations as an organisational function. However, **social media is still a big challenge for the PR industry itself**. That is why **this study aimed to research this new development and find comprehensive insights into what exactly happened and how should PR practitioners better approach new media opportunities.**

The age of 'we talk, you listen' style of company communication is gone; the dialogue with stakeholders is the only way forward, because the emergence of social media has changed the way consumers form opinions and make decisions (Flint, 2009). Therefore, many PR specialists, including Brown, Solis, Scott and others believe that **we are now at the peak of a magnificent era for the PR practice.** It also means that there are new tools and new techniques needed to meet client's needs and requirements. Butterick (2011) also mentions that the rise of digital media has transformed our channels of communication and the journalism practice (closely linked to PR), which in turn has had and will continue having an enormous impact on public relations.

As social media changes constantly, there is a continuous need to frequently investigate how social media is altering the PR practice which is the main justification and objective for this research. A first step in this study was examining a vast amount of recent literature sources. This critical review played the role of a basis to develop the following primary research and determine its focus according to the identified gaps in the literature. The report presents a number of existing evidence illustrating how greatly social media has changed and continues to change the PR industry.

Another purpose of the study was to examine the reasons for this phenomenon. To do so the research also aimed to investigate how practitioners themselves use

social media and how it has been integrated into the Marketing Mix. As Brown summarizes: "Now we are seeing altogether new ways of doing things and new things that we can do" (2009: 92), therefore **the research sought to identify these 'new ways' and 'new things' of how PROs work, but also to find out if social media has affected the private life of practitioners** in terms of e.g. if they now spend more time online 'working' in their free time. Furthermore, it was discovered in the literature that **measuring and monitoring SM and PR activities has been problematic for practitioners**, which is why this issue was another research objective.

Since this is **an industry level study** (Daymon and Holloway, 2002) the focus of the primary research was on professionals practicing PR in any area in order not to limit the research scope and **detect relevant findings about the whole industry hoping to provide new insights into the matter that would be of use for further research, but also for practitioners themselves to improve their knowledge and skills in SM.**

However, **a major difficulty was achieving a high enough response rate in the survey** because unfortunately the so needed support by the CIPR and PRCA was not able to be provided.

To gain an overview of the research Figure 1 presents the chapter disposition of the book and what each one includes, forming a logical structure for an easy read and digestion of the academic findings.

Figure 1: Book Overview

Chapter 1: Introduction

Highlights the project topic, reasons for and purposes of the research as well as the disposition of the book.

Chapter 2: Literature Review

Comprehensively examines PR and the industry, social media, the Marketing Mix and investigates social media's impact on PR in deep detail in order to critically review the literature and identify gaps.

Chapter 3: Research Methodology

Formulates the research objectives, paradigms and strategy in detail as well as the chosen primary research methods (survey and interviews) and the justification for these choices.

Chapter 4: Research Findings and Discussion

Presents the relevant data collected from both the survey and the conducted interviews, followed by a discussion that critically compares and contrasts the secondary and primary research findings.

Chapter 5: Conclusions and recommendations

Presents the conclusions drawn from the research findings as well as the limitations of the project and accordingly highlights recommendations for future research.

2. Literature Review

2.1. Public Relations

2.1.1. What is PR?

As a discipline, PR dates back to the beginning of the 20th century and is strongly linked to the growth of the media (print, TV, radio, online) when it begins to influence actions, behaviour and policy (Butterick, 2011).

In 1982 the Public Relations Society of America (PRSA, 2012) adopted the following definition:

> *Public Relations helps an organization and its publics adapt mutually to each other.*

Grunig and Hunt (1984: 8) similarly describe PR as **"the management of communications between an organisation and its publics."** The Chartered Institute of Public Relations (CIPR, 2012) offers another definition:

> *Public relations is about reputation - the result of what you do, what you say and what others say about you... It is the planned and sustained effort to establish and maintain goodwill and mutual understanding between an organisation and its publics.*

PRSA's definition has a strong implication on the importance of a dialogue, whereas the CIPR puts emphasis on reputation by building and fostering good relationships with various publics. Henslowe (2003) also highlights that PR is about establishing and maintaining a sound two-way communication between an organisation and everyone with whom it has any form of contact.

There are many more definitions of PR. The reason for this is that the industry itself is always changing and adapting to the world and growing power of the media, old and new (Gordon, 2011). However, most of them define it as **a discipline that is concerned with the exchange of information** (Phillips and Young, 2009) and as **a strategic management function that seeks to build relationships with the various publics of an organisation by maintaining a meaningful two-way communication with them**. It therefore should be an essential part of the organisational structure that can be truly effective when integrated into the broader business disciplines such as corporate planning, finance, HR etc. (Smith and Zook, 2011).

2.1.1.1. A New Definition is Needed

The emergence of new technologies and media in the last few decades have evoked a new era for the PR practice, which is why in November 2011 the PRSA launched the so called "Public Relations Defined" collaborative initiative, aiming to 'modernise' the existing definition (PRdefinition, 2011). From all candidates that the PRSA evaluated, a new definition was adopted in March 2012:

> *Public relations is a strategic communication process that builds mutually beneficial relationships between organizations and their publics.*
>
> PRSA (2012a)

2.1.1.2. Main Functions and Activities of PROs

According to Butterick (2011) **PR's primary function during the most of the 20th century was the attempt to get coverage in the media** for which the main ability was writing news releases that would serve their purpose to be used in the media. However, much has changed since then. Hence, Fawkes (2012) highlights the main responsibilities of PROs today as follows:

Table 1: Main PR Activities

Public relations activity	Explanation	Examples
Internal communications	Communicating with employees	In-house newsletter, suggestion boxes
Corporate PR	Communicating on behalf of whole organisation, not goods or services	Annual reports, conferences, ethical statements, visual identity, images
Media relations	Communicating with journalists; specialists; and editors from local, national, international and trade media, including newspapers, magazines, radio, TV and web-based communication	Press releases, photocalls, video news releases, off-the-record briefings, press events
Business-to-business	Communicating with other organisations, e.g. suppliers, retailers	Exhibitions, trade events, newsletters
Public affairs	Communicating with opinion formers (e.g. local/national politicians), monitoring political environment	Presentations, briefings, private meetings, public speeches
Community relations/ corporate social responsibility (CSR)	Communicating with local community, elected representatives, headteachers, etc.	Exhibitions, presentations, letters, meetings, sports activities and other sponsorship
Investor relations	Communicating with financial organisations/individuals	Newsletters, briefings, events
Strategic communication	ID and analysis of situation, problem and solutions to further organisational goals	Researching, planning and executing a campaign to improve ethical reputation of organisation
Issues management	Monitoring political, social, economic and technological environment	Considering effect of US economy and presidential campaign on UK organisation
Crisis management	Communicating clear messages in fast-changing situation or emergency	Dealing with media after major rail crash on behalf of police, hospital or local authority
Copywriting	Writing for different audiences to high standards of literacy	Press releases, newsletters, web pages, annual reports
Publications management	Overseeing print/media processes, often using new technology	Leaflets, internal magazines, websites
Events management, exhibitions	Organisation of complex events, exhibitions	Annual conference, press launch, trade shows

Source: Fawkes (2012: 10)

For the implementation of these practices new technology has offered new ways of communication such as Web 2.0 and social media (Fawkes, 2012). All these functions and the appropriate tools to fulfil them represent the **diverse nature of PR**.

2.2. The PR Industry

2.2.1. Growing Importance

The PR industry is nowadays an important worldwide multi-billion dollar industry and is regarded as an integral part of both businesses and governments (Corporate Watch, 2003). Just in the UK it is responsible for £6.5 billion turnover, employs 47,800 people, in-house, out-of-house in consultancies or as freelancers, and contributes ca. £3.4 billion to the country's economic prosperity and £1.1 billion to corporate profits (CEBR, 2005).

The importance of the profession has been remarkably influenced by the demand of the 24 hour media for content (Butterick, 2011). Various studies are expecting the future growth of the industry, especially in online and digital.

Figure 2: Areas of Greatest Growth in the Next Five Years

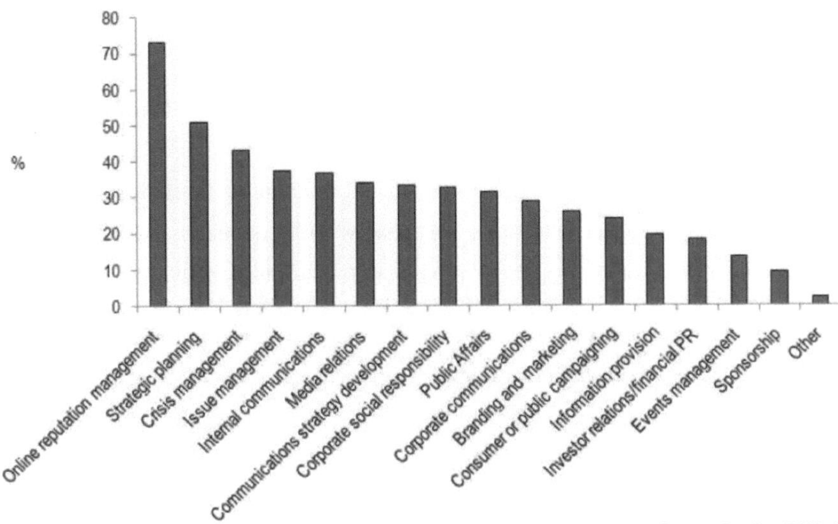

Source: ComRes (2010: 13)

Figure 3: European Communication Monitor's Three Year Growth Expectations

Today		In 2014		
1	Press and media relations: Print media	1	Online communication	↗
2	Online communication	2	Press and media relations: Online media	↗
3	Press and media relations: Online media	3	Social media	↑
4	Face-to-face communication	4	Face-to-face communication	→
5	Press and media relations: TV/radio	5	Press and media relations: Print media	↓

Source: Zerfass et al. (2011: 89)

2.2.2. Still Bad Reputation?

For years the industry's weakness has been its own reputation. **Many think of PR simply as 'spin' or 'propaganda'.** According to Davis (2007: 3) 'spin' is a synonym of "deceit, trickery or, at best, exaggeration, wishful thinking or fanciful interpretation." Often journalists and other influencers are unhappy with the "inauthentic, disingenuous, and "spamlike" ways of pitching them" (Solis and Breakenridge, 2009: 6).

Because of this many regard the industry as unethical (Brown, 2009). This, in turn, reflects to the major misunderstandings of the profession and lack of respect for it, which to some extent depend on the fact that there is still no equally recognised PR definition by all PR bodies. Nevertheless, according to Key Note (2007: 1) the industry is becoming more professional and is being considered as "the guardian of both brand and corporate reputation."

2.2.3. The Internet Evolution

Thanks to the Internet **communication is now possible anytime, anywhere**, no more just face-to-face. It is **instantaneous** and the importance of the geographical location is highly reduced (Davis, 2007). The Internet has now become primary information source.

Figure 4: Shocking Internet Statistics

2,357,504,433	Internet users in the world
202,941,501,029	Emails sent today
2,188,061	Blog posts written today
159,402,577	Tweets sent today
1,990,856,253	Google searches today

Source: Worldometers (16 April 2012)

Historically, PR used to provide the link between the supplier of a product, service etc. and its customer; now, it is the Internet (Phillips and Young, 2009). Press release distribution became easier, and cheaper – via emails (Yaxley, 2012). As The Cluetrain Manifesto (Levine, Locke, Searls and Weinberger, 2011) expresses:

> *A powerful global conversation has begun. Through the Internet, people are discovering and inventing new ways to share relevant knowledge with blinding speed. As a direct result, markets are getting smarter—and getting smarter faster than most companies. These markets are conversations.*

2.3. Social Media

2.3.1. Defining Web 2.0

Chaffey (2009: 22) defines Web 2.0 as "a collection of web services that facilitate interaction of web users with sites to create user-generated content and encourage behaviours such as community or social network participation, mashups, content rating, use of widgets and tagging." **One of the biggest advantages of Web 2.0 is that it allows UGC and mashups**, i.e. the ability to integrate content from different networks, e.g. Facebook can include YouTube videos (Phillips and Young, 2009). Moreover, **Web 2.0 facilitates a dialogue**, which also generates a much quicker and cheaper customer feedback (Smith and Zook, 2011). Solis and Breakenridge (2009: 2) argue that the Web 2.0, a term coined by Tim O'Reilly, was not only the "rebirth of the Web", but also a catalyst for the major changes happening to the PR industry.

2.3.2. Defining Social Media

Kaplan and Haenlein (2010: 61) define social media as a **"group of Internet-based applications that build on the ideological and technological foundations of Web 2.0, and that allow the creation and exchange of User Generated Content."**

Figure 5: Social Media Timeline

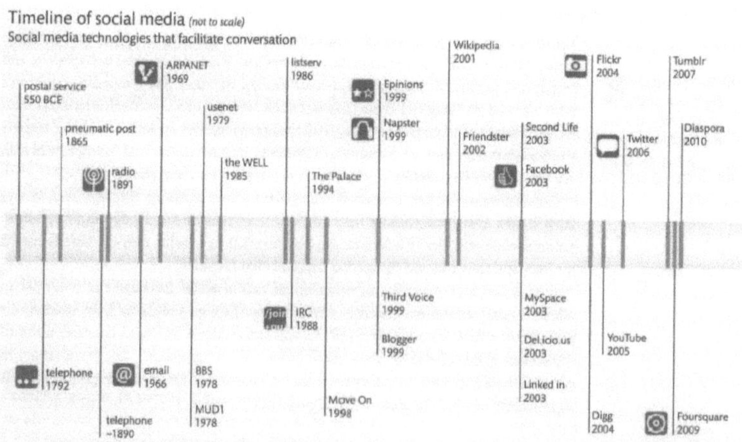

Source: Gordon (2011: 335)

Scott (2011) describes SM as the way **everyone can participate** by sharing ideas, thoughts and context and so can build relationships online, which is why he compares the term to a **'cocktail party'**. Similarly, according to Wikipedia (2012) **SM includes "web-based and mobile technologies used to turn communication into interactive dialogue"** through various forms such as magazines, forums, weblogs, micro-blogging, wikis, podcasts, pictures, video, rating bookmarking.

Figure 6: The Conversation Prism – Variety of Online Communication Channels

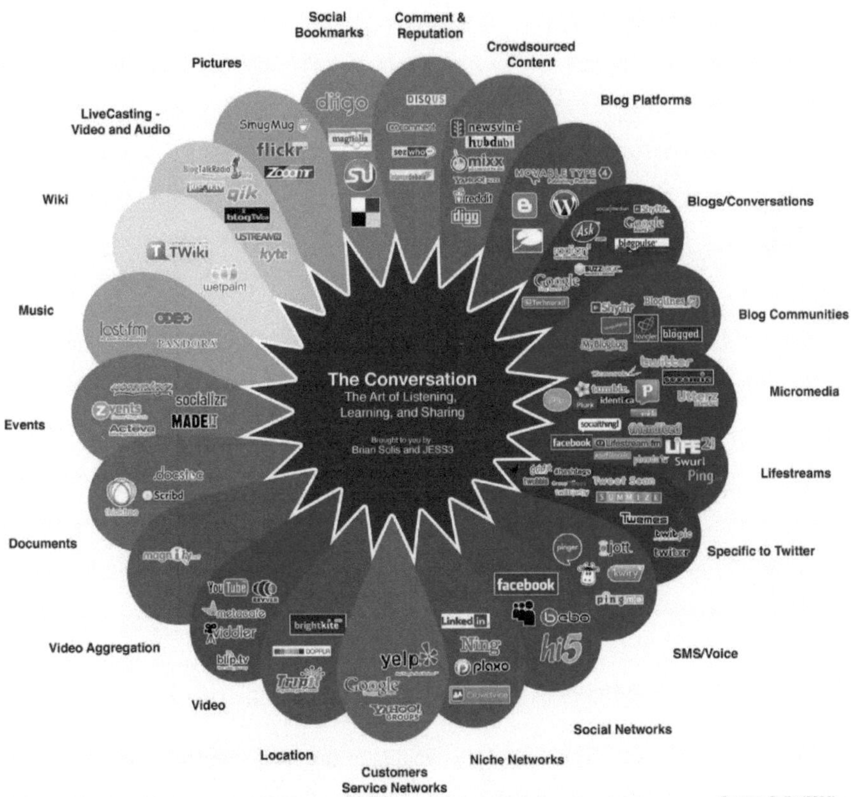

Source: Solis (2008)

Table 2: Basic Forms of Social Media

Social Networks	Allow people to build personal web pages and then connect with friends to share content and communication. The biggest social networks are **Facebook**, **LinkedIn** and **Bebo**.
Blogs	Perhaps the best known form of social media, blogs are online journals with entries appearing with the most recent first.
Wikis	These websites allow people to add content to or edit the information on them, acting as a communal document or database. The best known wiki is **Wikipedia**, the online encyclopaedia.
Podcasts	Audio and video files that are available by subscription, through services like **Apple iTunes**.
Forums	Areas for online discussion, often around specific topics and interests. Forums came about before the term 'social media' and are a powerful and popular element of online communities.
Content Communities	Communities which organize and share particular kinds of content. The most popular content communities tend to form around photos (**Flickr**, **Pinterest**), bookmarked links (**Delicious**) and videos (**YouTube**, **Vimeo**).
Micro-blogging	Social networking combined with bite-sized blogging, where small amounts of content ('updates') are distributed online and through the mobile phone network. **Twitter** is the clear leader in this field.

Source: adapted from Mayfield (2008: 6)

2.3.3. From Monologue to Dialogue

According to Brown (2009) people are engaging in the social web with others like them by not only consuming content, but also sharing ideas, interests and recommendations. Likewise, Solis (2011) also implies:

> *Social media is the democratization of information, transforming people from content readers into publishers. It is the shift from a broadcast mechanism, one-to-many, to a many-to-many model, rooted in conversations between authors, people, and peers.*

The advantage for brands by participating in those dialogues is that **engagement builds trust, relationships and loyalty, but on the other hand it also requires a "genuine, dedicated, proactive, and value-driven effort"** (Solis, 2007: 5). Even if organisations are not participating in the conversations, they are still happening, with or without them (Solis, 2011). **The time of the top-down communication is over; there is no longer just B2B or B2C communication, but B2C2B and C2C** (Brown, 2009).

Figure 7: Sending a Message through Traditional and New Media

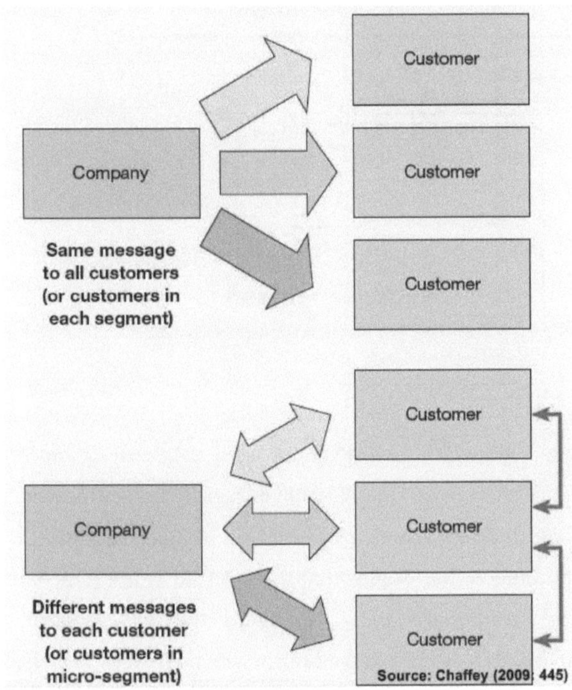

Social media and Web 2.0 have altered the entire media landscape by putting the power of influence in the hands of normal people who want to share their feelings, opinions and experiences (Solis and Breakenridge 2009a) and by this **new media plays the role of an extension of traditional word-of-mouth communication** (Hollensen, 2011; Mangold and Faulds, 2009).

Figure 8: Word-of-Mouth Opportunities with Social Media

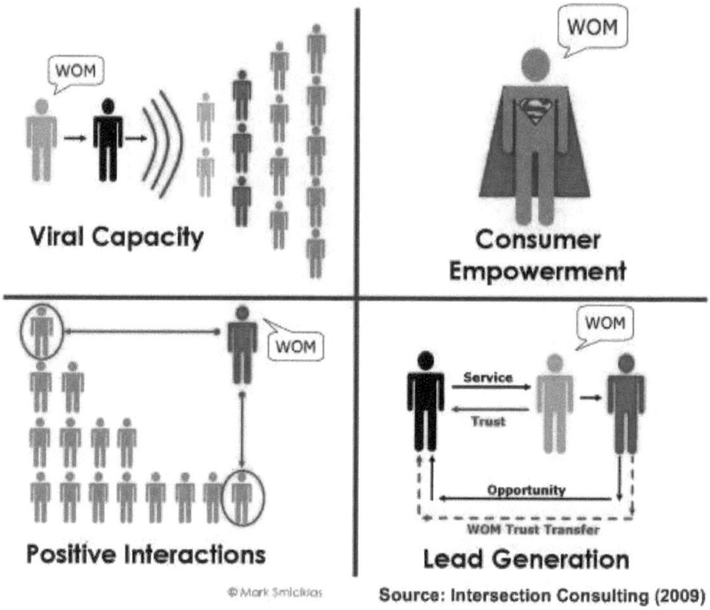

2.3.4. Traditional Media vs. New Media

Newspaper usage is declining – only 19% of Americans, aged between 18 and 34, **might** look at a daily newspaper (Butterick, 2011). TV is still engaging, but people have a wider choice and have found new, different channels to watch TV at their own time and disposition (Brown, 2009). The same author argues that the Internet is not a medium and is way more complex than traditional media, combining two very important 'features' – allowing traditional channels to migrate and reach new audiences as well as providing completely new media platforms where companies and customers can interact. **Information now seems to be coming to us rather than us finding it** (ibid).

Figure 9: The Online Media

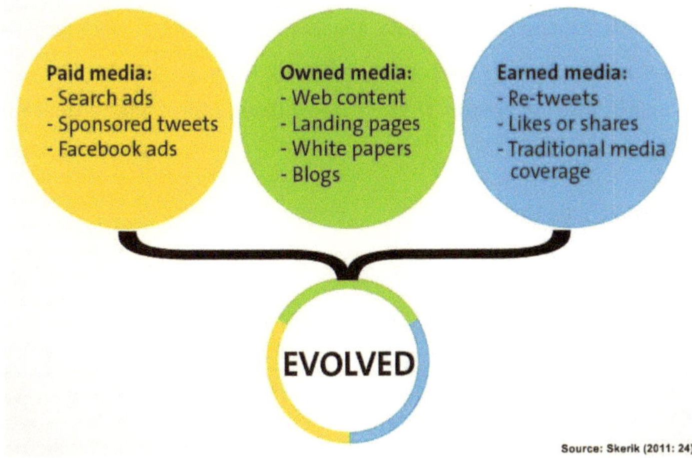

Source: Skerik (2011: 24)

2.3.5. Social Media Revolution and the 'Now' Factor

Social networking has now become the number one content category in worldwide engagement and accounts for 19 percent of all time spent online – this activity has more than tripled in the last few years (ComScore, 2012).

Figure 10: Time Spent Online on Key Internet Categories

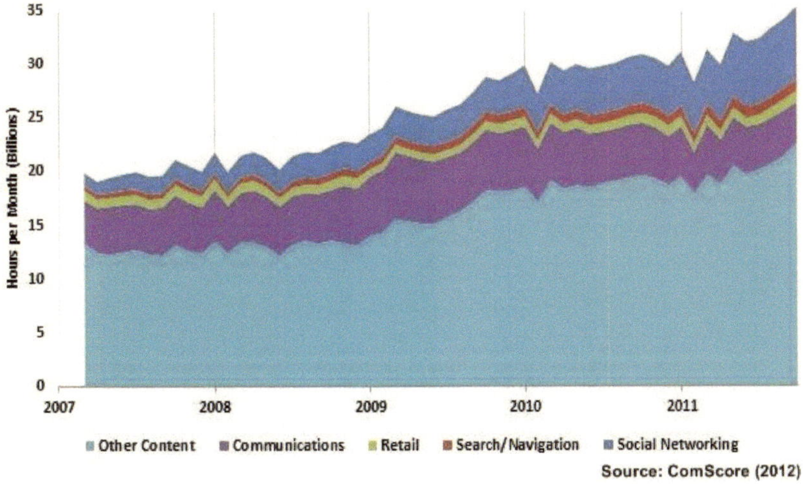

Source: ComScore (2012)

Twitter, for example, is now considered as a "news network" because it has become the distribution platform where news breaks first (Wallblog, 2011). In the same video Gerd Leonhard, a famous futurist and keynote speaker, expresses his opinion that Twitter will become even bigger than CNN because **it only takes ca. 40 seconds for news to be tweeted right after it breaks. In the case of Osama bin Laden's death it only took 26 seconds.**

Table 3: Interesting Social Media Facts

<table>
<tr><td colspan="3">• Adults spend more than 15 hours on the internet weekly.
• Social media has overtaken pornography as the number one activity on the net.
• Years to reach 50 million users: Radio – 38 years; TV – 13 years; Internet – 4 years; iPod – 3 years; Facebook added more than 200 million users in less than 1 year.
• Only 18% of TV ad campaigns generate positive ROI
• The average online video viewer watches 12.2 hours online videos a month.
• 133,000,000 – number of blogs indexed by Technorati since 2002.
• 34% of bloggers post opinions about products and brands.</td></tr>
<tr><th>Social network</th><th>Users</th><th>Interesting facts</th></tr>
<tr><td>Facebook</td><td>845 million</td><td>• The average user spends there more than 55 minutes/day.
• 60 million status updates daily.
• 2.7 billion Likes every day.
• 250 million photos uploaded daily.</td></tr>
<tr><td>Twitter</td><td>465 million</td><td>• 2-3 new accounts are activated every second.
• Ca. 175 million tweets a day.</td></tr>
<tr><td>Pinterest</td><td>10.4 million</td><td>• Accounts for 3.6% referral traffic now in comparison to July 2011 – only 0.17%.
• Average time spent by visitor – 97.8 minutes/month.</td></tr>
<tr><td>YouTube</td><td></td><td>• The 4th most visited site on the internet.</td></tr>
<tr><td>Wikipedia</td><td></td><td>• More than 14 billion articles by 75,000 contributors in 260 languages.</td></tr>
</table>

Source: adapted from InforCareITS (2011); TheTotalProfit (2011); Ragan (2012b); TheRealTimeReport (2012); PRDaily (2012); PRDaily (2012a); TheFutureBuzz (2009)

All this data indicates one very important aspect of SM – **things happen in real time; news breaks in seconds, not hours or days.**

2.3.6. Changing Consumer Behaviour

75% of consumers do not believe traditional advertising, whereas 71% are more likely to buy a product if someone referred to it on social media (Ragan, 2012). What is happening now is a "transfer of control, from the few to the many, from the corporations to the masses" (Brown, 2009: 157). Nevertheless, **SM still "feels like the Wild West" for many brands and they are not comfortable participating in an "environment where the consumer talks back"** (Brown, 2009: 16, 18).

Solis (2011a) calls this consumer influence 'collective intelligence' because:

> *Businesses are no longer the sole creator of a brand; it is co-created by consumers through shared experience and defined by the results of online searches and conversations.*

Today's consumer is not passive, but active and has multiple roles (Solis, 2011a).

Figure 11: The Roles of Today's Consumer

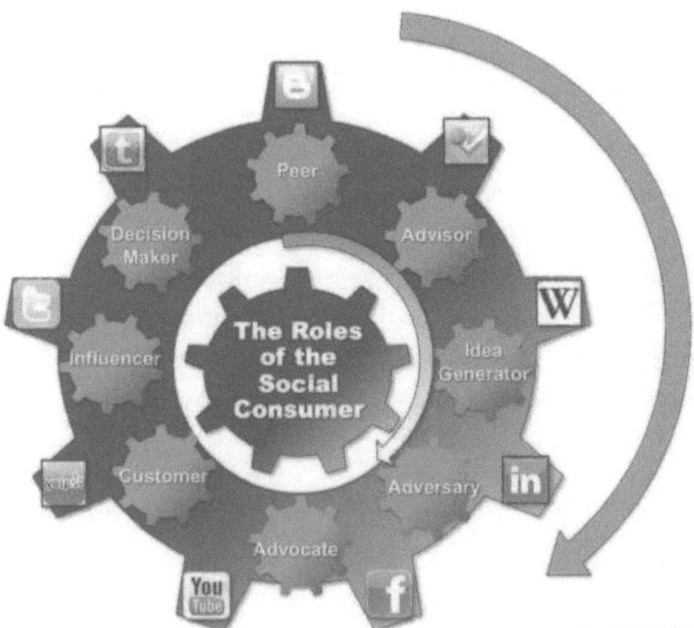

Source: Solis (2011a)

The biggest issue, however, is customer dissatisfaction being made public everywhere because dissatisfaction with a product, service or brand is usually expressed much more strongly than its counterpart (Brown, 2009). Nevertheless, even negative feedback can be 'positive' – companies can learn how to improve their products or services very quickly, but only of they listen to what their customers are saying.

2.4. Integrating PR and Social Media in the Marketing Mix

2.4.1. The Traditional Marketing Mix Today

In the Traditional Marketing Mix (Advertising, PR, Sales Promotions, Personal Selling and Direct Marketing) **PR was considered until the 1980s as just a support for marketing through media coverage and seen as 'free advertising' to encourage sales** (Davis, 2007: 13). However, the current shift from one-way towards two-way conversations and the increasing customer demands for constant interactions has given PR a considerable advantage over marketing, advertising etc. (Hutchinson, 2012) because it not only focuses on establishing relationships with the end users, but with all other stakeholders and therefore plays a huge role in reputation management (Butterick, 2011).

2.4.2. New Tools for the Traditional Marketing Mix

Marketers can no longer 'buy influence' (Brown, 2009: 85). Smith and Zook (2011: 4; 9) argue that social media is a 'game changer' because the customer has become a 'partner' who drives the business forward, i.e. has higher levels of involvement. They also argue that in order to actually allow this process, **marketers nowadays must integrate both the old 'outbound marketing' (advertising, direct mail, telemarketing etc.) and the new 'inbound marketing', which enables those conversations between the customer and the organisation to happen via social media.**

2.4.3. Integrated Marketing Communications

Integrated Marketing Communications (IMC) means "integrating all the promotional tools so that they work together in harmony…with one voice all the time" (Davis, 2007: 135). Here, effectiveness is the main advantage because **a message from a single channel has far less credibility than a message from multiple sources**

(Brown, 2009). In theory, such integration sounds credible; however, in practice it often happens that one of the elements, usually marketing or advertising, achieves the highest budget share, and the rest simply support this one aside (Fawkes, 2012). Nevertheless, **new technology and media are now being used across the boundaries of the communications mix**, namely for all promotion tools, because SM enables companies to better reach their target audiences well beyond the traditional media outlets (Tench and Yeomans, 2009). Reason for this is that social media replaces mass communication with networked relationships (Gordon, 2011). This necessary consistency of social networking with the use of the traditional IMC as a new paradigm results from the phenomenon that **SM is perceived by consumers as more trustworthy than corporate messages transmitted via the traditional mix** (Hollensen, 2011). Therefore, Mangold and Faulds (2009) argue that **social media is a hybrid element of the promotion mix that combines the traditional IMC characteristics (organisations talking to customers) on the one hand and an extended form of word-of-mouth (customers talking to customers) not controlled by marketers in terms of content and frequency.**

Figure 12: The New Marketing Communications Mix

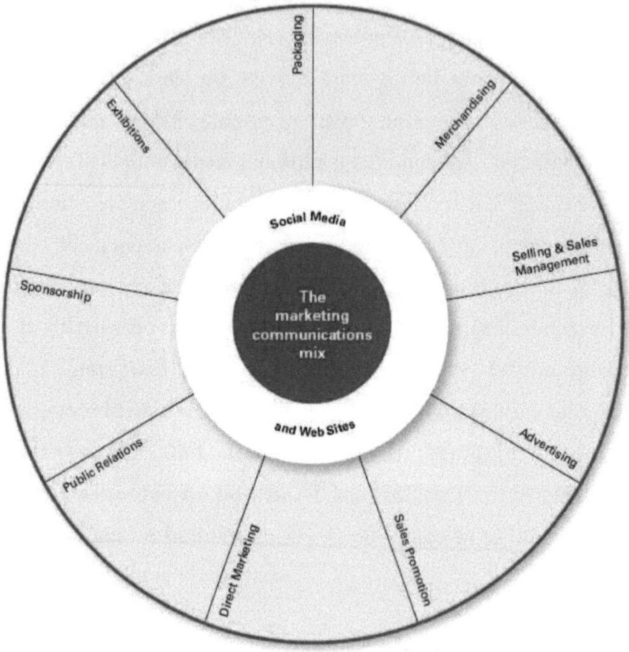

Source: Smith and Zook, 2011

2.5. Social Media's Impact on PR

According to Richard Edelman, CEO of the world's largest independent PR consultancy Edelman, social media has altered "the nature of how we do what we do" (Curiosity, 2012). It is a **'shift from pitching to participating, from selling a story to telling a story'** (Solis and Breakenridge, 2009a).

Table 4: Impact of Social Media According to PR Practitioners

2007	*2008*	*2009*	*2010*	*Statement*
58%	*61%*	*73%*	*83%*	Agree blogs and social media have changed the way organisations communicate.
53%	*59%*	*68%*	*81%*	Agree the emergence of social media and blogs has changed the way organisations handle external communications.
	75%	*85%*	*88%*	Agree social media and blogs compliment mainstream media.

Source: adapted from Wright and Hinson (2010)

2.5.1. How about PR Theory?

Many claim that the emergence of social media has changed both PR theory and practice. **New technologies have allowed the practice to better develop a dialogue with its publics, evolving towards Grunig's two-way symmetric communications model** (Theaker, 2012).

Table 5: PR Communications Models

	Model			
Characteristics	***Press agentry/ publicity***	***Public information***	***Two-way asymmetric***	***Two-way symmetric***
Purpose	Propaganda	Dissemination of information	Scientific persuasion	Mutual understanding
Nature of communication	One-way; complete truth not essential	One-way; truth important	Two-way; imbalanced effects	Two-way; balanced effects
Communication model	Source → Rec.	Source → Rec.	Source → Rec. ← Feedback	Group → Group ←
Nature of research	Little; 'counting house'	Little; readability; readership	Formative; evaluative of attitudes	Formative; evaluative of understanding
Where practised today	Sports, theatre, product promotion	Government, non-profit associations, business	Competitive business; agencies	Regulated business; agencies
Estimated % of organisations practising today	15	50	20	15

Source: adapted from Fawkes (2012a: 35)

Figure 13: The New Grunigian View of Modern PR

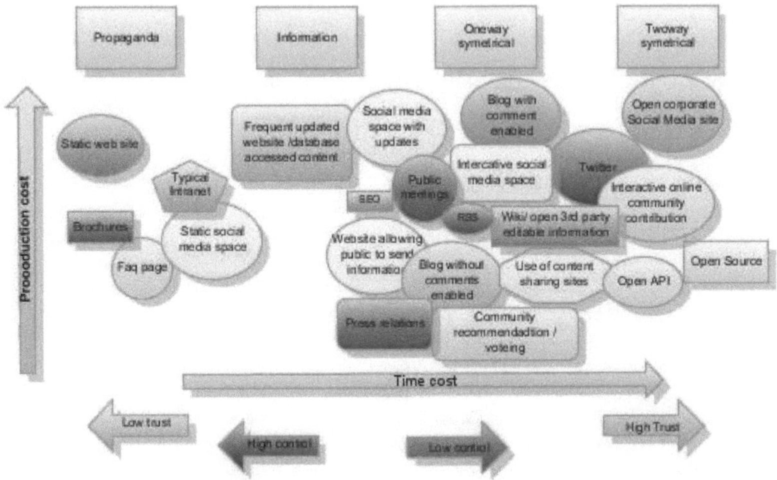

Source: Phillips (2009)

2.5.2. Impact? How? Why?

Solis and Breakenridge (2009a) argue that **what actually caused the reinvention of PR by social media was UGC. It changed the "dynamics of influence" and put the power in the hands of ordinary people** (Solis, 2011). Therefore, PROs must now engage in the conversation through the various new channels and tools. In this sense, Solis and Breakenridge (2009a) furthermore argue that in the world of Web 2.0, **content is no longer king, but conversation is.**

Marshall McLuhan, a Canadian professor in English literature and a philosopher, once proclaimed: **'the medium is the message'. Nowadays, the medium has become the message** (Brown, 2009) because SM provides PR with additional channels to instantaneously communicate with target publics (Franklin, 2009).

Brown (2009) calls the described new development a 'communications upheaval' more significant than the printing press. According to the author **companies themselves used to decide on a desired image and PR had to just present it. Now, however, they have lost that control and this image is directly built by the consumers.**

Scott (2011) explains, **PR used to be almost only about media relations** – if you had a good story, you had to pitch it to a reporter; then if he/she liked it, he/she would write about it and so people would find out what is happening with organisations. Today, companies can directly and in real time communicate with buyers and other influencers on multiple social media platforms (ibid). **Reaching target audiences has become easier not only locally, but also globally.** Furthermore, many journalists do not just wait to receive press releases, but find these on their own on the Social Web.

Figure 14: Most Important Research Methods for Journalists

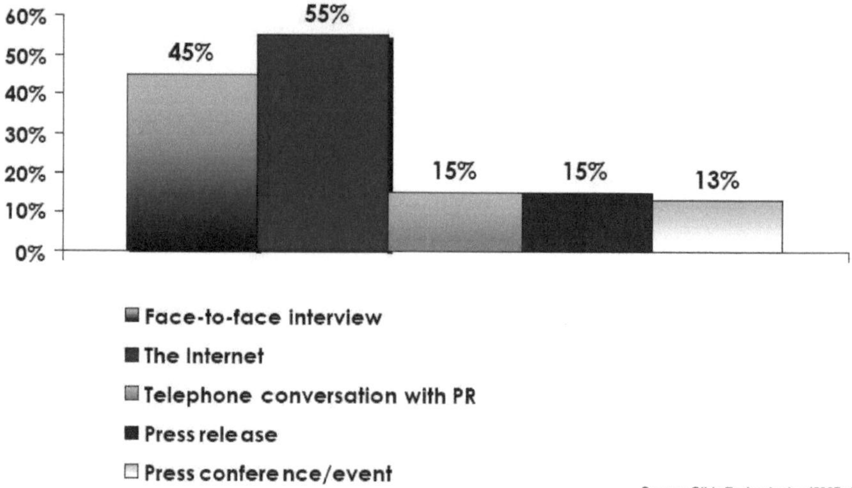

Source: Glide Technologies (2007: 4)

On the other hand, in terms of PR **UGC can often be considered to have an inbuilt credibility gap** (Tench and Yeomans, 2009). There is a **lack of control of what is being said online**, which is a major concern for PROs and organisations (Gordon, 2011). PR professionals can only partially control UGC by designing and hosting websites, wikis, blogs, Facebook and Twitter presence etc. and trying to engage with consumers to react (Guth and Marsh, 2012). Still, the demand for 24 hour stories and content in the media is a major challenge for the industry (Butterick, 2011).

2.5.3. What is New PR?

Solis and Breakenridge (2009a) offer the following definition for new PR:

> *PR 2.0 is the realization that PR now has an unprecedented opportunity to not only work with traditional journalists, but also engage directly with a new set of accidental influencers. We can now talk with customers directly (through social networks, wikis, micromedia communities, online forums, groups, blogs, and so on)... New PR's goal is to understand the communities of people we want to reach and how to engage them in conversations without marketing at them.*

Figure 15: New Model of PR

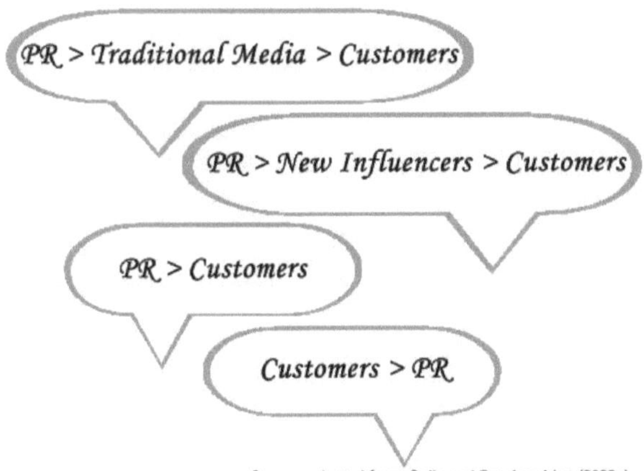

Source: adapted from Solis and Breakenridge (2009a)

Table 6: The Old vs. the New Rules of PR

Old Rules	*New Rules*
• The only way to get ink and airtime was through media. • Companies communicated to journalists via press releases. • Nobody saw the actual press release except a handful of reporters and editors. • Companies had to have significant news before they were allowed to write press releases. • Jargon was okay because the journalists all understood it. • You weren't supposed to send a release unless it included quotes from third parties, such as customers, analysts, and experts. • The only way buyers would learn about the press release's content was if the media wrote a story about it. • The only way to measure the effectiveness of press releases was through clip books, which noted each time the media deigned to pick up a company's release. • PR and marketing were separate disciplines run by different people with separate goals, strategies, and measurement techniques.	• PR is far more than just a mainstream media audience. • You are what you publish. • People want authenticity, not spin. • People want participation, not propaganda. • PR is not about your boss seeing your company on TV. It's about your buyers seeing your company on the web. • The Internet has made public relations public again, after years of almost exclusive focus on media. • Companies must drive people into the purchasing process with great online content. • Blogs, online videos, e-books, news releases, and other forms of online content let organisations communicate directly with buyers in a form they appreciate. • Social networks allow people all over the world to share content and connect with the people and companies they do business with. • On the web, the lines between marketing and PR have blurred.

Source: adapted from Scott (2011: 11-12, 23-24)

2.5.4. Social Media Activities, Tools and Skills for PR professionals

Social networking has become a PR pro's personal operating system (Solis, 2011). Hence, PR must learn to listen and correspondingly respond forgetting about traditional pitching and moving forward to conversation-based interactions that form personalised relationships. To do so, Solis and Breakenridge (2009a) point out that PROs should master new activities such as blogger relations, social media releases, corporate blogging etc.

Figure 16: Online PR activities

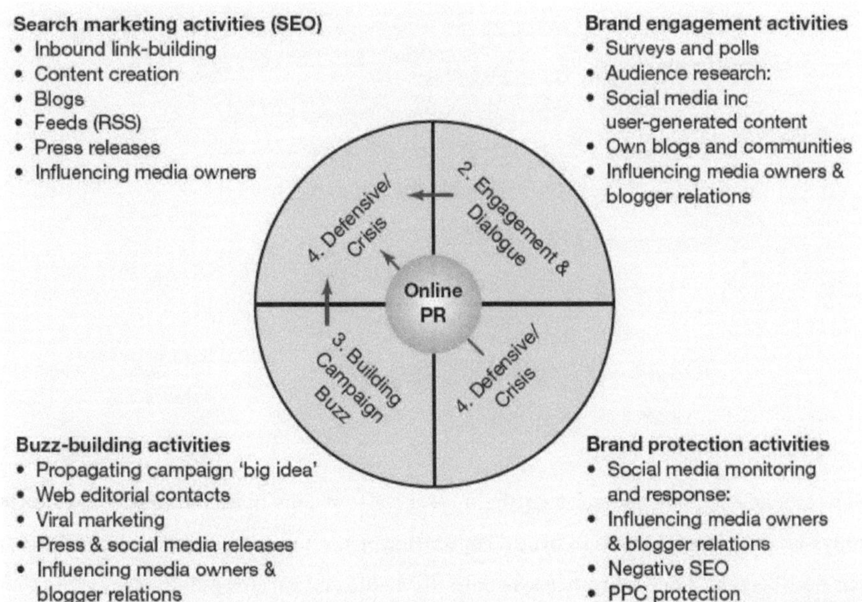

Source: Chaffey (2009: 515)

PR is no longer just about audiences, but about people; not just about new tools, but about relationships because **"in the social economy, relationships are the new currency"** (Solis and Breakenridge, 2009a). PR practitioners have to 'go' where customers are, using the appropriate channels to reach them; those channels now still include both traditional and new media (ibid).

Figure 17: Usage of Social Media Channels by PROs

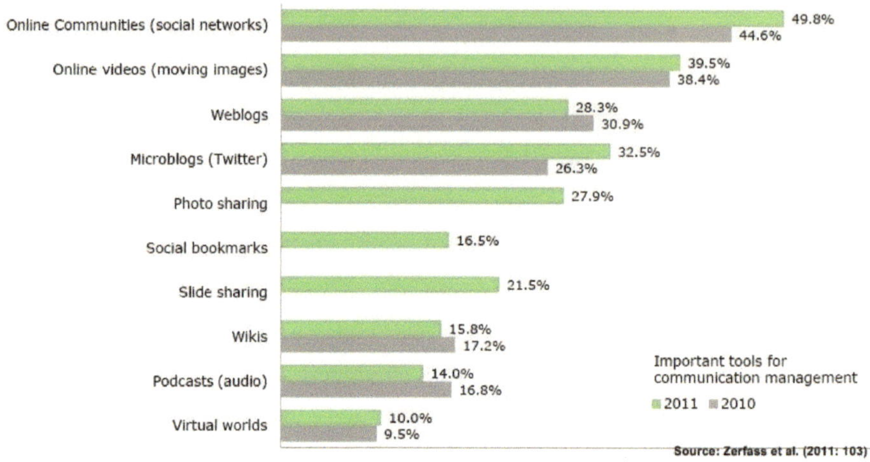

For companies losing control over the message also means that **customer experience plays an ever greater role in brand reputation.** Therefore, corporate communications has now become a necessity, because both the media and various publics are asking a lot more questions and a lot more often than ever before (Henslowe, 2003).

Figure 18: The New PR Skills

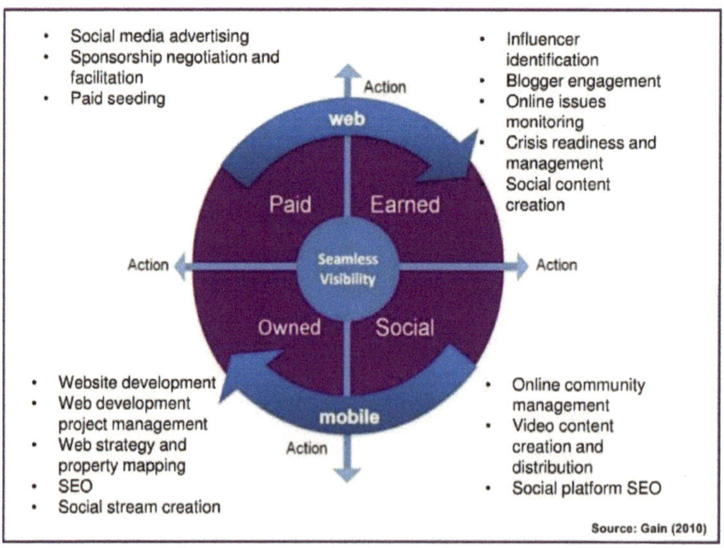

Because of the vast amount of new communication platforms, there are no longer just traditional releases, but also customer-focused releases, SEO releases, social media releases and video news releases (Solis and Breakenridge, 2009a). Furthermore, as a primary information source, online search is still extensively happening and has led to the emergence of a new PR skill – search engine optimisation (SEO), predominantly content driven (Yaxley, 2012).

Table 7: Media Relations vs. Blogger Relations

	Traditional journalism	*Blog journalism*
Narrative style	Detached	Personal
	Neutral	Opinionated
	Both sides	One-sided
Approach to audience	Audience as passive recipient	Audience as co-creator
Story form	Structured format (e.g. inverted pyramid)	Fragments
	Answers basic questions (who, what, etc.)	Incomplete
	Closed text	Open text
	Sources and datelines credibility	Hyperlinks for credibility

Source: Phillips and Young (2009: 216)

However, this variety of channels has made it difficult for PROs to determine which ones are most influential and effective. Furthermore, the number of active users on the various networks indicates an information overload which makes it even harder to engage and make an impact (Yaxley, 2012). **This complexity results into difficulties measuring and monitoring PR activities** which makes it even harder for the industry to prove its effectiveness.

2.5.5. And in Reality – How is Social Media being used by PR Professionals?

According to Key Note (2007) there is a **lack of skilled and trained professionals**. Many practitioners admit that social media has had a huge impact on PR, but just a few feel confident employing SM strategies for PR. **In CIPR's Benchmarking Survey, 23% of members admitted that their knowledge of SM was limited** (ComRes, 2010).

Table 8: Percentage of Average Working Time PROs spend with Blogs and SM

	None	*1%-10%*	*11%-25%*	*26%-50%*	*More than 50%*
2009	7%	48%	30%	11%	4%
2010	4%	38%	34%	17%	7%

Source: Wright and Hinson (2010: 19)

Table 9: Importance of Social Media for the Overall PR Efforts

How important is each of the following in the overall communications and public relations efforts of your organization (or your client's organizations)?

	Very unimportant			**Somewhat unimportant**			**Uncertain**			**Somewhat important**			**Very important**		
	2009	*2010*	*2011*	*2009*	*2010*	*2011*	*2009*	*2010*	*2011*	*2009*	*2010*	*2011*	*2009*	*2010*	*2011*
Blogs	13%	11%	12%	17%	22%	22%	11%	10%	11%	41%	39%	40%	18%	18%	14%
Electronic Forums or Message Boards	13%	14%	21%	24%	28%	30%	16%	17%	17%	37%	30%	28%	10%	10%	4%
Podcasts	21%	24%	28%	21%	32%	30%	21%	17%	17%	30%	24%	21%	7%	5%	4%
Search Engine Marketing	10%	8%	9%	9%	15%	13%	19%	13%	13%	29%	46%	38%	32%	5%	27%
Social Networks (Facebook, Linkedin etc.)	14%	5%	4%	16%	9%	6%	17%	9%	7%	39%	47%	48%	13%	30%	36%
Micro-Blogging Sites (Twitter etc.)	22%	8%	7%	19%	15%	10%	25%	12%	11%	26%	42%	46%	8%	23%	26%
Vide Sharing (YouTube etc.)	16%	9%	6%	13%	13%	10%	18%	13%	13%	38%	43%	46%	14%	22%	25%

Source: adapted from Wright and Hinson (2011)

In the European Communication Monitor, many practitioners admitted that social media is still a big challenge (Zerfass et al., 2011) mainly because they cannot keep up with all new platforms being introduced constantly, which also represents a difficulty deciding on which to focus.

Figure 19: Social Media Skills and Knowledge of PROs

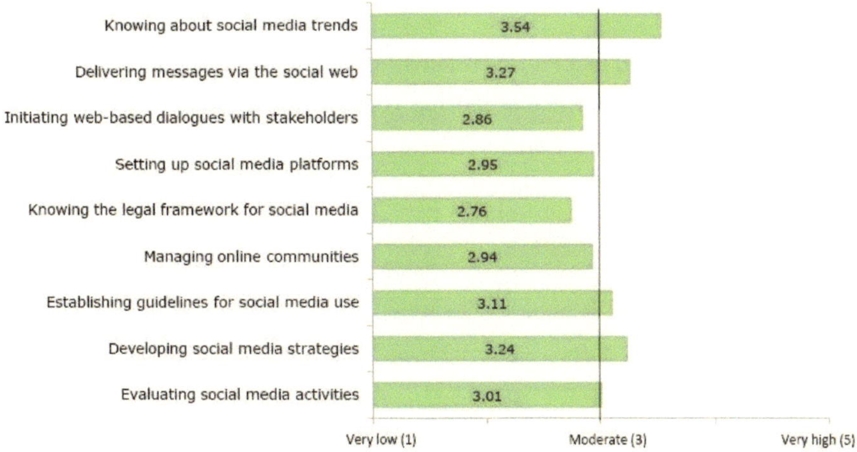

Source: Zerfass et al. (2011: 100)

Another reason, as Solis and Breakenridge (2009a) point out, is that **many PROs simply do not 'bother' to take time to build those relationships and engage with the public. A role in this also plays the poor use of those channels in their free time.**

Figure 20: Private Use of Social Media by PROs

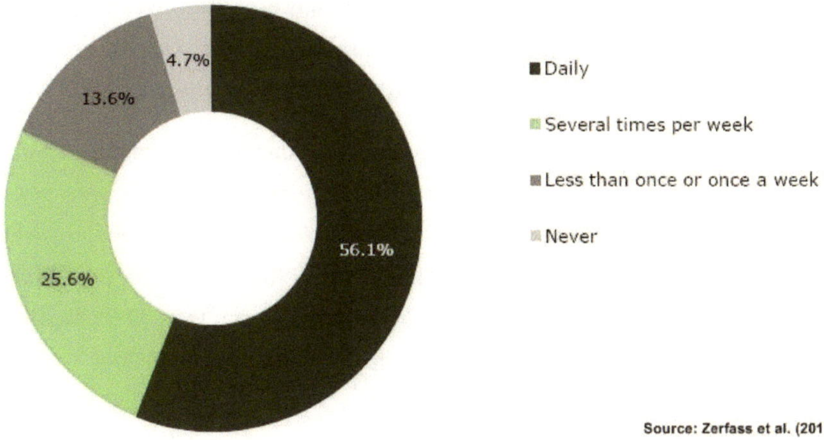

Source: Zerfass et al. (2011: 105)

Many say social media should be measured; howeve, just a few are actually doing so (Wright and Hinson, 2010) – for example, only 21% of organisations measure the ROI of their SM efforts (Society for Human Resource Management, 2012). As Scott (2011) points out, the problem is that **PR practitioners still only measure traditional media, but forget to evaluate the 'value of sharing' content online.** Companies still rely too much on 'imperfect' influence scores such as Klout[3] or PeerIndex[4] that do not really tell anything about how **digital influence** is actually created and used (Solis, 2012). Some tools, as for example Google Analytics[5], Facebook Insights[6], Google Alerts[7], Radian6[8] etc. (PRDaily, 2012b), have been gaining importance among practitioners. However, those predominantly focus on quantitative findings, whereas PR has a lot to do with qualitatively orientated efforts – e.g. forming opinions – that are hard to measure and evaluate.

2.6. Conclusions

Many authors and many researchers have been examining the influences of the Social Web on PR. They all agree **SM has altered the PR practice because it has enabled a better reach of target audiences and a direct, real-time communication that builds relationships**. PRSA's annual surveys for example provide valuable insights into the quantitative side of the matter. **However, it would be interesting to also perform a more in-depth research and illustrate the implications of the new trend on the life of PR practitioners, both working and personal, e.g. what exactly are their activities and how much do they interfere with their private sphere.**

Because of the very nature of social media, i.e. constantly changing, all the discussed implications must be researched on a very regular basis. New social networks are emerging every year and some of them have a major influence on the PR practice, e.g. Pinterest or the new Facebook Timeline. **PROs cannot be sure which communication channels, tools and platforms will be relevant in 2020** (Phillips and Young, 2009). Examining social media's impact on the PR industry in 2016 for example

---

[3] http://klout.com/
[4] http://www.peerindex.com/
[5] www.google.com/analytics/
[6] https://www.facebook.com/insights/
[7] http://www.google.com/alerts
[8] http://www.radian6.com/

would show very different results than today (2012) because **the media landscape is evolving all the time.**

While these literature sources very well present the changes that happened and highlight what PR practitioners should be doing, it seems that utilising social media is still a big challenge. **The lack of knowledge in SM, which in turn reflects all current measurement difficulties, suggests that the exact same matter on SM's impact on PR will be of interest for quite a while in the future in order to research the causes for the shortage of skills as well as the measurement issues and how to find the best solutions to solve them.** Nevertheless, the indicated literature is an excellent starting point to understand the new PR industry.

3. Research Methodology

3.1. Research Objectives

The research seeks to investigate, describe, analyse and explain how social networking and online platforms such as Facebook, Twitter etc. have altered the Public Relations industry during the past few years and the way and for what purposes PR specialists are using those new tools and channels. This means that **the research is of exploratory and descriptive nature**, i.e. is trying to portray and clarify an understanding of a specific issue (Saunders, Lewis and Thornhill, 2007). With regards to the defined research objectives and according to the identified gaps in the literature the following main research questions (RQ) were formulated:

RQ1: How has the emergence of social media changed the PR practice – is it a positive or a negative impact?

RQ2: How and why are PR practitioners using social media in their working activities on the one hand, and in their free time on the other?

RQ3: Why measuring and monitoring PR and social media activities are a big issue and what tools do practitioners utilise to solve this?

3.2. Research Philosophies and Paradigms

Historically, the world of PR knowledge and research has been dominated by the positivist (or realist) view (Daymon and Holloway, 2002). The reality is therefore independent of the ones involved in it and would rely on objectivity (ibid). This, in turn, is characteristic for quantitative studies where generalisation is possible. However, as the research seeks to also examine how PROs themselves think social media impacted PR, i.e. personal opinions, and what their working and personal experiences in terms of it are, another paradigm is of importance, namely **interpretivism** (or phenomenological paradigm). It emphasises that the research is conducted among people rather than objects because they themselves are 'social actors' (Saunders, Lewis and Thornhill, 2007: 106). Therefore, the best suited approach is the **inductive approach** by first collecting and analysing data and after that formulating a hypothesis (ibid).

3.3. Research Strategy

In accordance with the discussed objectives and paradigms a **mixed method research** that combines both quantitative and qualitative techniques was chosen (Saunders, Lewis and Thornhill, 2007). Such research strategy promises maximum results because it integrates statistical data such as rate of social media usage by PROs with detailed explanations of the viewpoints and opinions of practitioners with regards to their working and personal life. Therefore, a **self-administered survey** that seeks to identify the needed numerical data in combination with **in-depth interviews** that focus on words and meanings were selected as **the most suited methods**. These two, in turn, are also the most popular and easy to conduct research techniques and most appropriate considering the time frame and resource limitations. Furthermore, a questionnaire offers to make generalisations and to move from general to specific (Collis and Hussey, 2009), where the latter would provide an easy link to the following interview findings.

Table 10: Distinctions between Quantitative and Qualitative Data

Quantitative data	Qualitative data
• Based on meanings derived from numbers	• Based on meanings expressed through words
• Collection results in numerical and standardised data	• Collection results in non-standardised data requiring classification into categories
• Analysis conducted through the use of diagrams and statistics	• Analysis conducted through the use of conceptualisation

Source: developed from Dey (1993); Healey and Rawlinson (1994), cited in Saunders, Lewis and Thornhill (2009: 482)

3.4. Research Methods

3.4.1. Quantitative Methods

A survey contributes to providing knowledge descriptive in nature, i.e. offers statistical description, which is one of the research purposes (Business Research, 2012). This cannot be achieved using other quantitative methods such as for example an experiment that seeks to find a causal relationship between two variables (ibid, 2012a). Because of the time constraints of the research **an important advantage of conducting questionnaires is that they are least time-consuming, but they nevertheless provide easily comparable data because of the standardised questions.** The idea behind this method is to support the in-depth data gathered from the interviews with statistical findings. **An online survey was preferred for its facile distribution and implementation.**

Table 11: Advantages and Disadvantages of Questionnaires

Advantages	Disadvantages
• Low cost • Fast • Efficient • Contingency questions effective • Direct data entry • Wide geographic reach	• Coverage bias • Reliance on software • Too many digital surveys, causing overload

Source: Sue and Ritter (2012: 5)

3.4.1.1. Survey Structure and Design

Typical feature of quantitative research is a structure, where questions are determined before the beginning of the primary research (Daymon and Holloway, 2002). Since the survey was targeted at PROs active in the profession and therefore have a rather busy working life, the **questions were designed as forced-choice questions with predefined answers** (De Vaus, 2002). However, for most of them it was optional to leave comments and explanations. It was decided upon a small number of questions (only 10) in order to facilitate a higher participation rate (Appendix 1). **The focus of the questionnaire was on RQ1 and RQ2** in order to gain statistical insights into these matters. Another reason for this, as stated in the conclusion of the literature review, is that even though this topic has been researched before, it is necessary to be regularly examined because of the constantly changing social media landscape. The questionnaire does not seek to find answers on RQ3 simply because of the very nature of the question, namely to answer "Why?" which requires a discussion.

Many surveys have problems with their complexity, which was a key issue to be avoided so that more responses could be collected. **To encourage participation, the questionnaire was specifically designed and worded to be easily and quickly completed and was anonymous.** Survey Monkey was the chosen software because of its usage simplicity, large number of options for question design and the fact that it is free.

After the questionnaire was designed there was an **initial pilot testing**, where the survey was posted in a few LinkedIn groups and left there for a week. After responses were analysed some small technical and design issues were identified and corrected. **Furthermore, the questionnaire structure, questions type and formats were discussed via email with a PR expert with more than 30 years of experience in the industry, which helped improve the quality of the survey**.

3.4.1.2. Sampling and Survey Distribution

The minimum sample size was set at 50 in order to be representative; the actual achieved number was 80. The chosen sampling technique was non-probability sampling, and more accurately **purposive sampling of a homogeneous group of people in a particular subgroup with similar members**, namely people working in the PR industry (Saunders, Lewis and Thornhill, 2007). **This sampling technique was both informative and suited for a smaller sample size**.

The initial idea was to ask the CIPR and the PRCA to send the survey link to their members; however, this was not possible. Therefore, to achieve statistically valid results, the web link was distributed via email to PR practitioners with the kind help of some of the interviewees and other PR contacts of the researcher. Furthermore, Plymouth Chamber of Commerce was asked to send the questionnaire link to their PROs contacts. The survey was also posted on various groups in LinkedIn such as the CIPR, PR Professionals etc. where members of the groups were asked to participate. To increase awareness, the questionnaire was promoted via Twitter as well. This data collection process took place in March 2012 for two weeks.

3.4.2. Qualitative Methods

Qualitative methods are associated with the 'interpretive worldview' and allow exploring people's intentions, motivations, beliefs and experiences (Daymon and Holloway, 2002: 4). **As the most suited technique for exploratory and descriptive researches it was decided upon conducting interviews** (Saunders, Lewis and Thornhill, 2007) and since the research is qualitative this is where the main focus would lie on. Having used focus groups or observation as methods would not have provided enough in-depth data relevant to the research topic.

Table 12: Advantages and Disadvantages of Interviews

Advantages	Disadvantages
• Good response rates • Can ask complex questions • Longer interviews may be tolerated	• Limited geographic reach • Time-consuming • Expensive • Susceptible to interviewer basis • Sensitive topics difficult to explore

Source: Sue and Ritter (2012: 5)

3.4.2.1. Interview Structure and Design

Two pre-planned, semi-structured face-to-face interviews and five structured asynchronous email interviews, both types based on similar eight questions, were conducted (Appendix 3). Key areas of this method focused on **comprehensively answering all RQs**. The main **advantage of the semi-structured interviews was the so called 'evolving conversation'** with rather spontaneous questions and reactions (Daymon and Holloway, 2002: 167), which allowed discovering additional important data for the research topic and made observation possible. **The structured email interviews** on the other hand not only allowed participants to find enough time to respond, but since the questions were pre-determined, it was **easier to compare the responses and identify similar patterns**. Furthermore, the geographical distance with this technique was irrelevant.

Key issue was the wording of the questions so that there were **no leading or ambiguous, but clear and easy to understand queries**. The structure and design of the interview was pre-tested by the researcher by giving answers and recording the necessary length of response time, which was planned to be ca. 30 minutes having taken into consideration the participants' valuable time.

3.4.2.2. Sampling and Conduction of Interviews

The usual norm for qualitative researches is a rather small sample size (between four and forty participants) because they are concerned with providing rich and detailed explanations (Daymon and Holloway, 2002). The chosen sampling technique was a mix of homogeneous and convenience sampling of potential participants with the same type of experience, namely in the PR industry (ibid). **Interview participants were selected so that they work in different areas of the practice, have various educational**

backgrounds and are based in the UK. The idea behind this was to find out if there would be any differences in viewpoints in accordance with participants' occupational role – in-house, out-of-house in a big and a small organisation or as a freelancer. This is how sufficient and relevant information was able to be generated and thereby the sample was representative of the population (Sekaran and Bougie, 2009). Ideally, the researcher would have preferred to have conducted interviews with key members of the CIPR (such as the CEO etc.); however, this was not possible. Therefore, the researcher had to contact other PR practitioners to meet the planned sample.

The initial sample size was five in-depth interviews, however in the end there were seven respondents, because only two were possible to be face-to-face. **Nevertheless, the point of saturation, where no new data emerged, was reached** (Daymon and Holloway, 2002).

The face-to-face interviews were conducted according to participant's availability and were recorded. Email ones were distributed online and respondents had one month to answer the questions and send their responses back to the researcher. These took place in February and March 2012.

3.4.3. Consideration on Ethical Issues

The following guidelines were adopted in order to ensure an ethically sound research (Daymon and Holloway, 2002: 78):

- The right of free and informed choice.
- Protection from harm – no emotional or physical risks.
- Principles of privacy: anonymity and confidentiality.

All interview participants received the same brief explaining the research purpose and some details about the researcher. They were politely asked if they were willing to take part in it and/or if they had the time, and were not pressurised. The same was introduced in the emails sent to PR practitioners to fill in the survey and on the LinkedIn posts. **Participation in both was voluntary. Confidentiality and anonymity was ensured** for both: the questionnaire was completely anonymous; the interviewees were attentively asked if they allowed to be accredited or if they preferred for their names, experience and educational background not to be mentioned. Two participants wished to stay anonymous and for some data to remain confidential, which was kept. In general, no problems occurred.

3.4.4. Conclusions

As social media is a relatively new development, the proposed research aims to increase knowledge on the subject by providing comprehensive explanations about the topic. Therefore, **combining both quantitative and qualitative methods offered an 'added dimension' to the examination**, because the survey results represented a broad picture on the issues, whereas the in-depth interviews gave a more detailed perspective (Moore, 2006: 13). This suggests that **both approaches complemented each other for optimum results**. Furthermore, using both methods provided the advantage of obtaining high correlation among the collected data through all sources and thereby led to **more credibility** to the whole research (Sekaran and Bougie, 2009), but also **higher validity and explanatory power of the data** (Fielding, Lee and Blank, 2008). **Most importantly, mixed method researches "appear to be gaining a foothold in the communication, marketing and management literature"** (Daymon and Holloway, 2002: 9).

4. Research Findings and Discussion

4.1. Quantitative Data Findings

The questionnaire was distributed as discussed in the previous section. 80 respondents completed the survey so that **the pre-planned sample size was achieved and even exceeded**, which suggests that **the promotion of the questionnaire was adequate.**

First step of the analysis was **data preparation**, initially beginning with **data editing** (Sekaran and Bougie, 2009). Minimal missing data was discovered in question 10 due to a small researcher technical mistake with the software; however, this was easily corrected. Nevertheless, all other questions were fully responded because no opt-out option was allowed. Some **data cleaning for the optional open-ended questions** was also performed so that it is error-free and there are no odd results (Moore, 2006) – for example answers like "N/A" were not considered. Additionally, these comments required **coding**, so that the responses were classified in **specific categories** with their own similarities (ibid). To help identify them the **software for qualitative data Weft QDA** was used (see next section) and the **Online Text Analysis Tool**[9] that allows to very quickly find the most frequent phrases and words. The data was then exported into Microsoft Excel to allow easier analysis and presentation of the findings in a suitable analytical manner by first illustrating the respondents' profile and then moving towards to the specific findings with regards to the survey's research objectives – RQ1 and RQ2.

4.1.1. Participants' Profile

To gain a broad understanding of the sample the last section of the survey (questions 8, 9 and 10, Appendix 1) was concerned with **profiling the participants in accordance with their experience in the industry, current employment and occupational role.** Important to note is that this was an online survey so that the sample was not able to be controlled. However, these questions enabled to ensure the participation only of PR practitioners at least to a certain extent.

Nearly 40% of the respondents have been working in PR for one to three years, whereas the next two larger participant groups were the ones with between 4 and 10

[9] http://www.online-utility.org/text/analyzer.jsp

years (ca. 26%) and those with more than 20 years of experience, accounting for almost 14%.

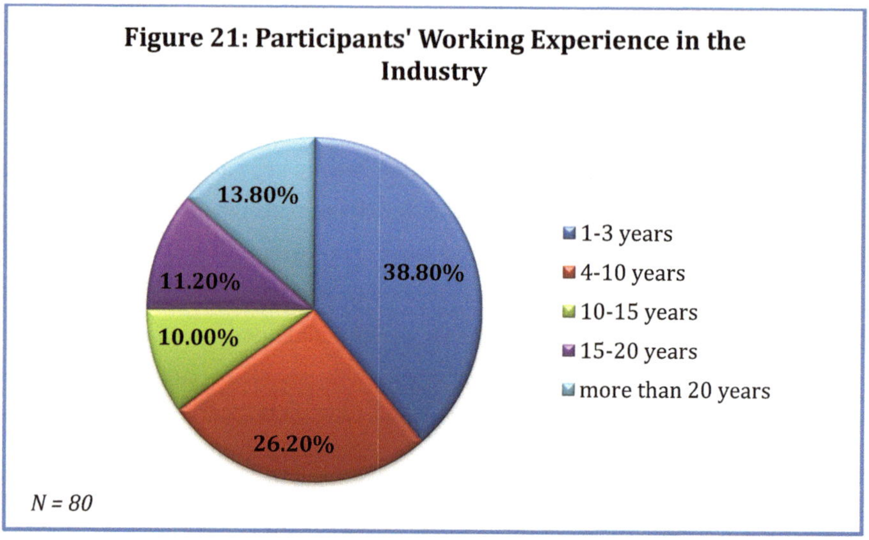

Even though the majority of the respondents have been in PR for a fairly short time and therefore have not experienced the difference between PR now and PR before the emergence of social media, still more than 30% of the participants have witnessed those changes first hand. **Nevertheless, as the social media landscape is constantly changing the experiences of both are equally important and relevant for the research**.

The next two questions were concerned with the respondents' occupational role and employment. As Figure 22 displays, almost **half of the respondents work in-house**, i.e. in the PR or communications department of an organisation. This, indeed, is not a surprise because according to CEBR (2005: 14) ca. 80% of all PROs in the UK are employed directly by a company.

Figure 22: Participants' Organisational Employment

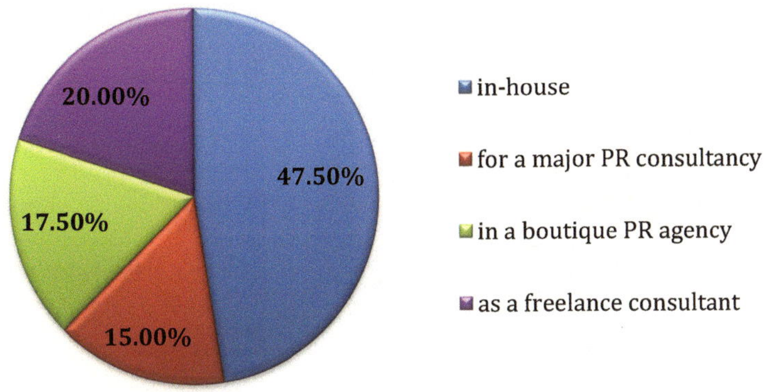

N = 80

Interesting is the fact that the **respondents that work for large PR consultancies account for the smallest amount**, but because the market is highly dominated by major worldwide organisations a higher number was expected.

In correspondence with the first query in this section, not surprisingly about 22% of the participants are in the beginning of their PR careers and 35% work either as Account Executives or Account Managers, which normally are the ones with at least 4-10 years of experience. **These results, in turn, are an indication of the sample's reliability**.

Figure 23: Participants' Current Occupational Role

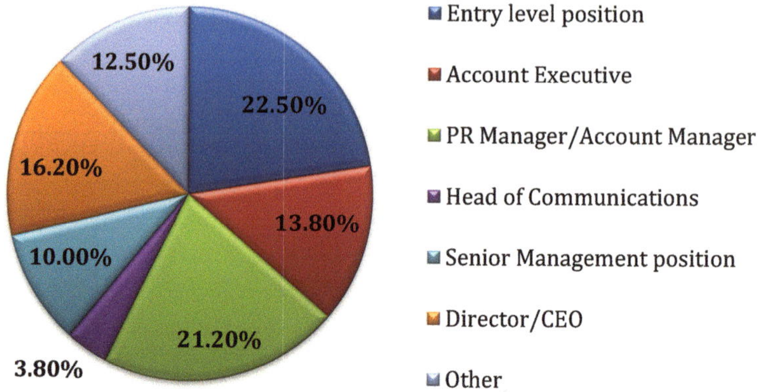

N = 80

About 16% of the respondents said they are responsible for the role of a Director or CEO, which indicates their experience in the industry and thereby **increases the quality of the research**. Other occupational roles specified by the participants were University Lecturer, Educator or Professor, Editor & Co-owner of a newspaper; Communications Consultant, PR & Communications Officer, Press Fleet and Events officer, PR & Marketing Research Professional, Communications Assistant.

The questionnaire did not ask for name, age or contact details because it adhered to the ethical standards outlined in the previous section and also because this data would not have been of any particular use for the research.

4.1.2. RQ1: Impact of Social Media on the PR Industry

This section of the survey started with a general and sort of an introductory question interested in finding out what the role of social media for PR according to practitioners was. All respondents but one agree that **SM has enhanced the practice**, which is indeed a significant number.

Figure 24: Has Social Media (including Blogs) enhanced the PR Practice?

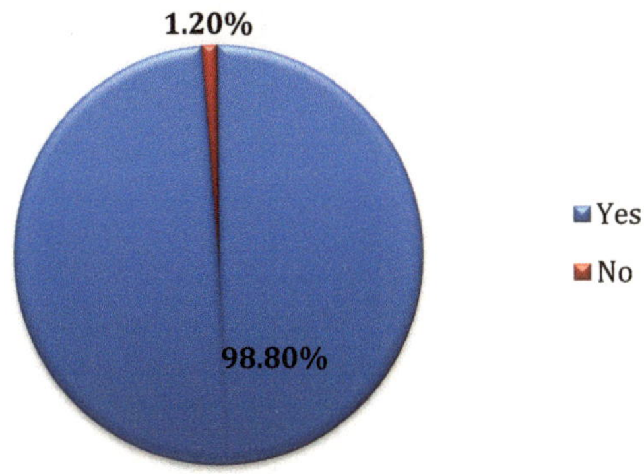

N = 80

There was an optional field for participants to leave comments about how exactly SM has a positive or a negative impact on the practice. Respondents have indicated a number of positive reasons and no negatives (see Figure 25). In general, **social media has "opened up a whole world of communication possibilities."**

Figure 25: Reasons for SM's Positive Impact on PR

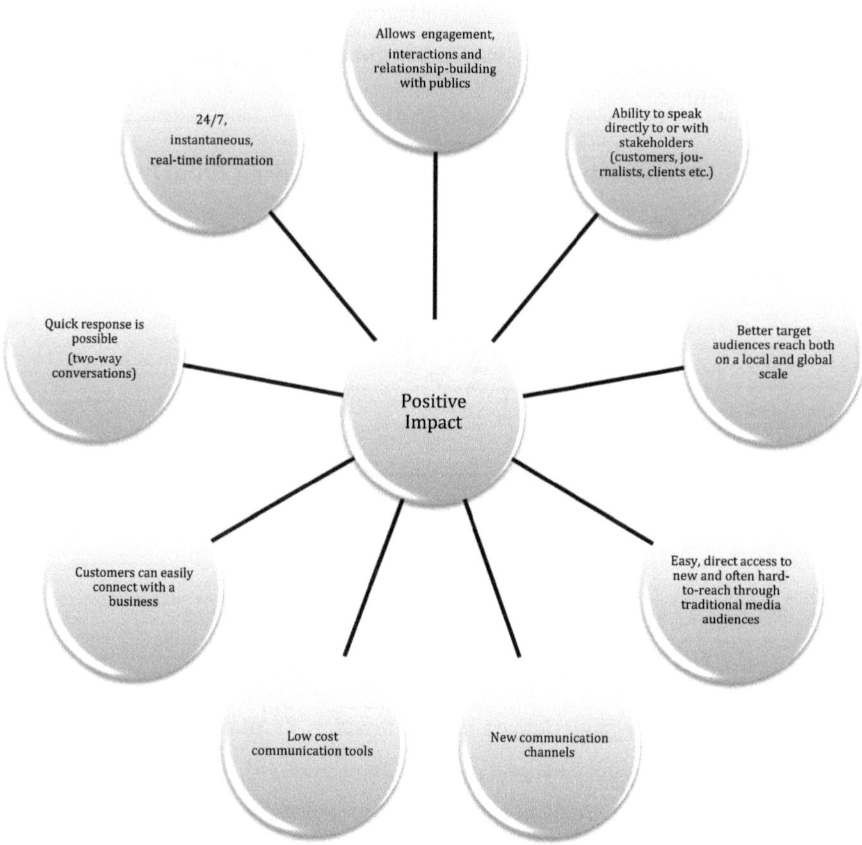

When asked what PROs think about social media's trustworthiness as a news channel about 60% believe it is even **more accurate and reliable than traditional sources** such as newspapers, TV or radio.

Figure 26: Accuracy and Reliability of Social Media in Comparison to Traditional Media (Newspapers, TV, Radio etc.)

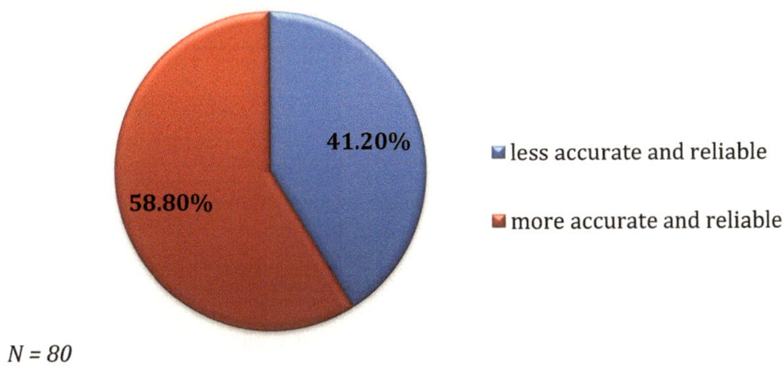

The optional open question here was concerned with the reasons for this. The comments indicate an interesting debate where many **respondents believe that this is not necessarily a definite Yes/No question**, because **accuracy and reliability depend rather on the source itself**. Others, on the other hand, suggest that **SM is more trustworthy because of the high amount of first-hand, quick and direct information**. Additional reasons for both Yes and No are illustrated in Figure 27.

Figure 27: Accuracy and Reliability of Social Media

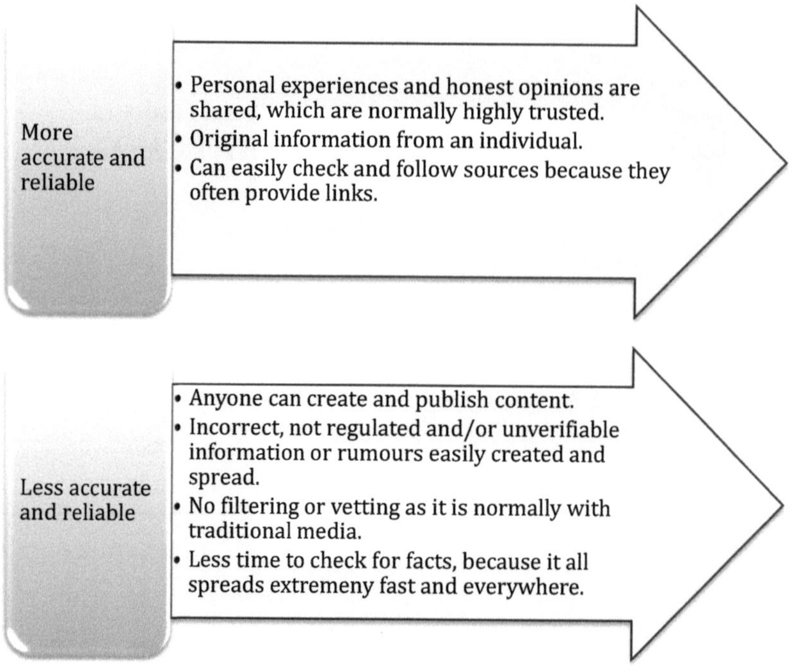

The financial perspective of the usage of social media is of particular importance for a number of companies, especially in times of economic crisis or recession. The majority of the participants (77.50%) stated that **SM activities are much more cost effective** for developing relationships with various publics in contrast to traditional media.

Figure 28: Cost Effectiveness of Social Media Activities for Developing Relationships with Various Organisational Publics

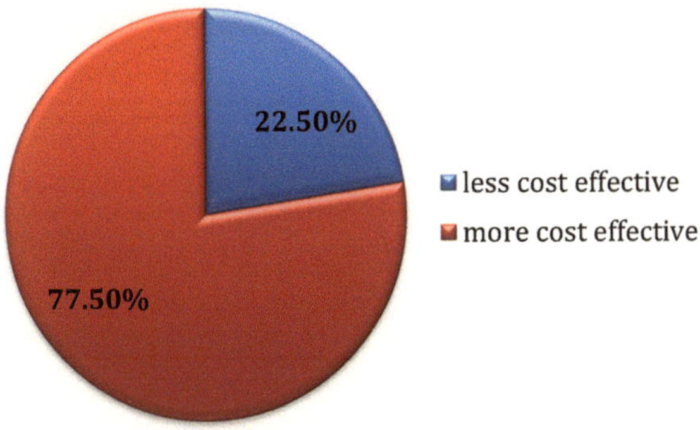

N = 80

Participants advocate this **cost effectiveness** mainly because **social media is cutting edge, can be used anytime and anywhere, allows better audience reach and interactions and often publics come to you.** However, many indicate that this is so **only if done right**, which in turn requires a lot of effort, qualified personnel and time ("time is money"), and that it very much **depends on the industry, campaign, its objectives and publics.**

4.1.3. RQ2: Social Media Usage by PR Professionals

The next section of the questionnaire was concerned with the rate of SM usage by PROs and the adoption of tools for PR activities. **Practitioners rank Facebook as the most important social media channel for organisational PR efforts** – almost 30% share this opinion. Considering that Facebook has ca. 850 million active users (Facebook Newsroom, 2012) this is not much of a surprise.

Figure 29: Importance of Social Media Platforms in Priority Order for the Overall Organisational PR Efforts

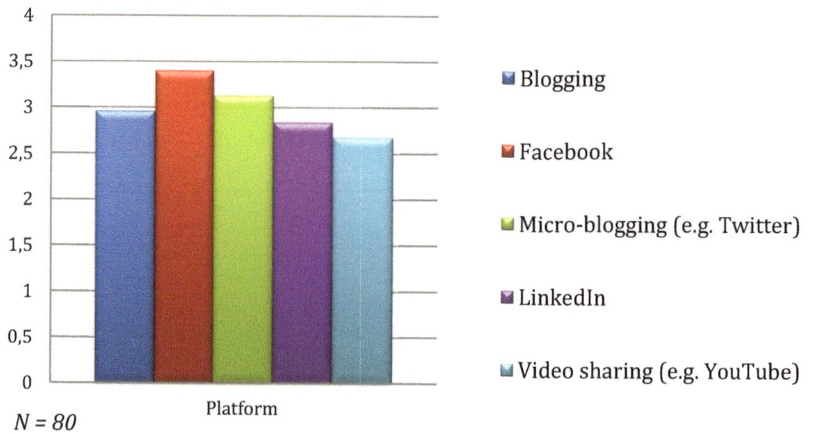

Significant roles play micro-blogging platforms such as Twitter, closely followed by **blogging** activities. **Least important for PROs here are LinkedIn and Video sharing channels** such as YouTube, which indeed is not unusual because LinkedIn mainly serves as a business contact network, whereas YouTube is often an entertainment platform (see below). Pinterest[10], online newspapers, Foursquare[11], photo sharing site (e.g. Flickr[12]), company website, Quora[13] and Slideshare[14] are other channels that according to participants are important for the organisational PR activities.

---

[10] www.pinterest.com
[11] www.foursquare.com
[12] www.flickr.com
[13] www.quora.com
[14] www.slideshare.net

The next two questions sought to identify the **differences in social media usage by PROs in their working activities** on the one hand **and in their free time** on the other. As shown in the following two figures, **practitioners use Facebook and Twitter very frequently in both occasions** - almost 44% admit using Facebook and 55% Twitter at work and ca. 62% and 45% respectively are active there in their spare time. A surprise here was that **blogging appears to be a least favourite and utilised activity** - ca. 28% blog somewhat infrequently at the office and 25% never do in their free time, which contradicts to the fact that blogging is considered one of the most important activities for the organisational PR efforts as indicated above. PROs are **not that active on YouTube** either. Interestingly, **practitioners are using LinkedIn more at home (ca. 40%) than at work (30%).**

Figure 30: Frequency of Social Media Platforms Usage in PROs' Day-to-Day Working Activities

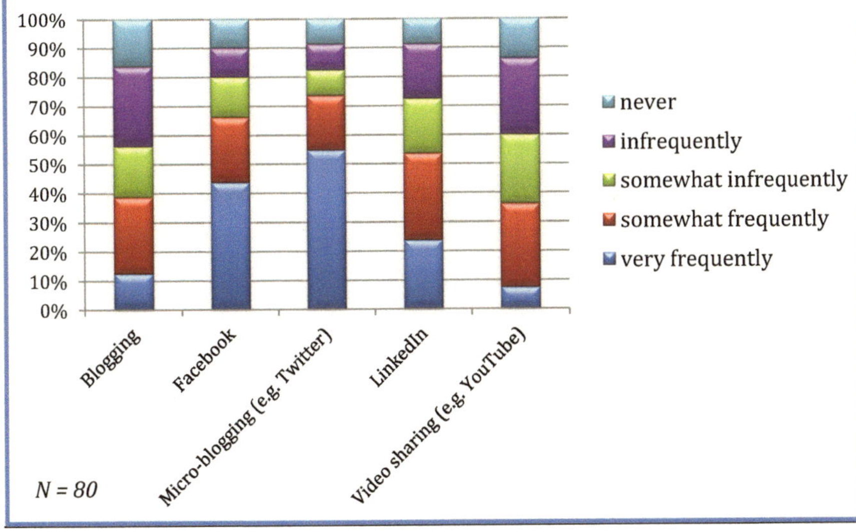

Figure 31: Frequency of Social Media Platforms Usage in PROs' Free Time

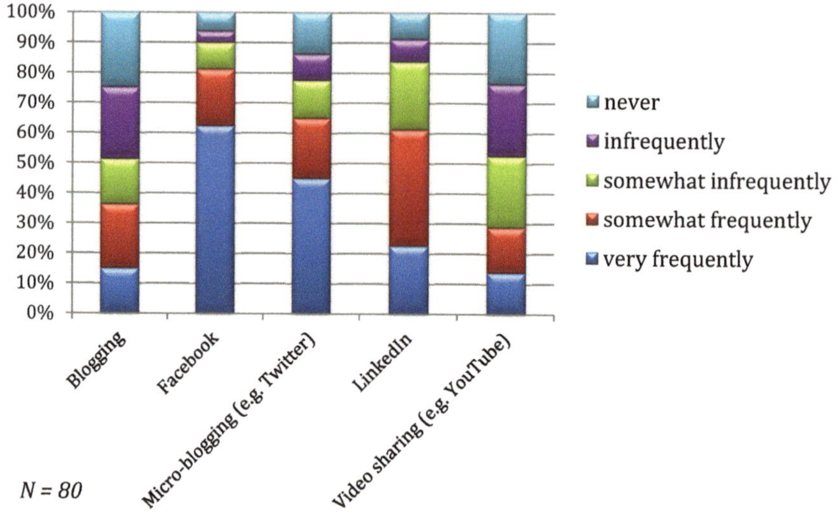

The last question tried to create a link to the previous two questions and to make clear what the reasons for the mentioned rate of SM usage above were. The high activeness in **Facebook** in practitioners' free time can be explained by the fact that they rather use the network for **social interactions with friends and family** – almost 84% admit to do so – or to share and create content (ca. 43%). **Twitter**, on the other hand, they utilise **to stay up-to-date with for example news and trends** (ca. 63%), **to enhance business relations with e.g. clients or journalists** (ca. 57%) or to share and create content (ca. 50%). Almost 72% admit that **LinkedIn is a platform that helps enhance business relations.** YouTube they (ca. 40%) utilise for sharing and creating content.

Figure 32: Purposes of Social Media Platforms Usage

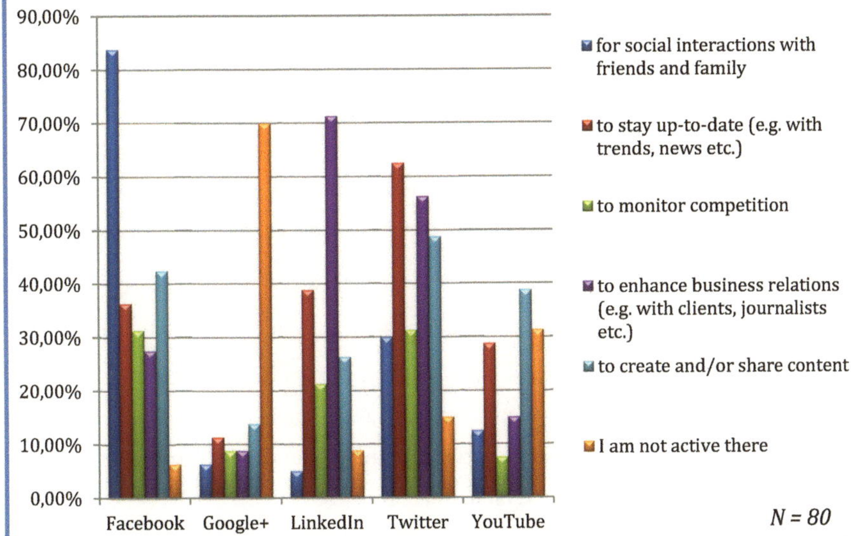

An interesting fact is that even though **Google+** has been around for almost a year, **PROs have still not adopted it – 70% are not active there at all**. Another peculiar finding is that apparently **PR professionals are not really using SM platforms to monitor competition** – only about 30% admit to do so just in Twitter or Facebook.

4.2. Qualitative Data Findings

The qualitative data was analysed using the free, open-source software Weft QDA chosen because of its ease of use, which was an important issue for the researcher working with such software for the first time, and because it includes some standard CAQDAS[15] features (Fenton, 2006). **It was decided upon using such a programme also because of the large amount of qualitative data that was collected** (see Appendix 4). Additionally, the Online Text Analysis Tool was used here too for a fast, broad perspective on the matters.

The **first step here was data editing and reduction**, where data was selected and coded, which helped drawing meaningful conclusions by **identifying patterns and relationships between perceptions** (Sekaran and Bougie, 2009). **Data was then systematically segmented into categories around the main RQs so that it could be easily as well as thematically analysed and compared** (Moore, 2006).

4.2.1. Participants' Profile

As discussed in the Research Methodology, **UK PR professionals from various industries, educational backgrounds and current occupational roles** were targeted (for more information on each participant see Appendix 4). In general, almost all participants have made a big contribution to the industry during their years of work experience – for example Rob Brown is author of the book "PR and the Social Web", which was intensively referenced in the literature review, so was Alison Theaker's (another interviewee) "The Public Relations Handbook", a fundamental read in PR studies.

---

[15] Computer assisted qualitative data analysis software

Figure 33: Interview Participants According to Current Occupational Role

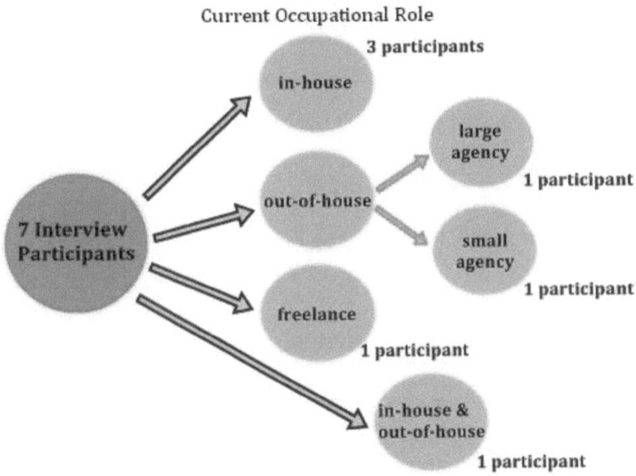

4.2.2. RQ1: Impact of Social Media on the PR Industry

In order to find comprehensive answers about how exactly the emergence of social media altered PR the first four questions focused on the following categories:

Figure 34: Main Categories for RQ1

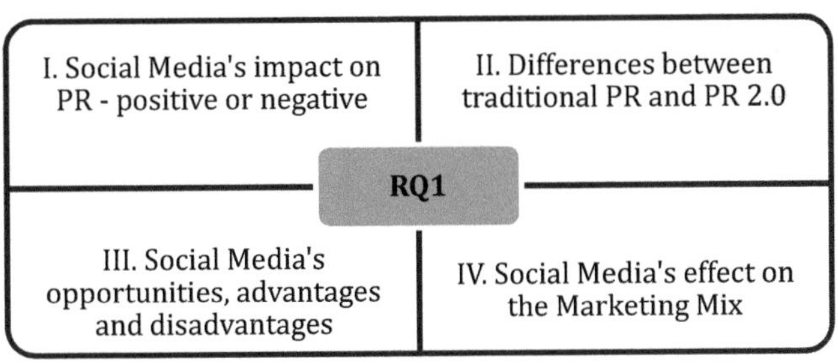

There were **two opposite opinions of practitioners about issue I.** Some believe **SM has changed PR to "an absolutely massive extent"**, because "social media has opened a huge amount of channels for us, it has introduced a lot of new audiences that we would not have been able to engage with before; it has enabled PR professionals to 'go global' in terms of reach and influence" (Appendix 4, Interview 4) and has made the industry "more reactive than ever before" (Appendix 4, Interview 6). Others argue that **it has**

simply provided new channels and tools for the practice, but PR remains fundamentally the same. In regards to this, Alison Theaker said: **"If you were doing good PR before that [SM], it doesn't make a difference. For good PR people digital changes nothing"** (Appendix 4, Interview 5). Nevertheless, all agree that there are changes, positive as well as negative, as shown in Table 13.

Table 13: Positive and Negative Changes for PR due to SM

Positive	Negative
• SM provides new, disintermediated channels for organisations to interact in personal ways with whole groups of people. • Sending messages without relying on traditional media to carry it for you is now possible. • SM has helped engaging in a dialogue. • Opportunities to reach new audiences, locally and globally. • Opportunities to talk directly with rather than to publics and to listen to what they are saying. • Opportunities to more easily get customer's feedback. • Time and location do not matter. • Everything is much quicker, even instantaneous. • Individuals can share their own content. • Great internal communication tool; employees can engage with organisations.	• Everything is public now; there is nowhere to hide. • Major demanding and unforgiving accountabilities if you ever make a mistake. • Reputation issues – if something does not go well, it will spread wildly and fast on SM. • No control over social media. • A lot more difficult to manage issues and crisis situations. • Everyone can now be a publisher, editor and journalist - more inaccuracies. • SM has replaced face-to-face communication a little bit.

From a business perspective **"social media has changed the way organisations interact with their stakeholders**... those stakeholders hold them to account very publicly and to all parts of the world at any time... **PR has a major advisory role** to enable senior managers to understand how SM works, why they cannot ignore it and what new obligations it lays on them" (Appendix 4, Interview 2).

When asked about issue II, Shelley Fletcher shared her view (Appendix 4, Interview 7), which very much summarised the differences between PR now and then as follows:

> *The main difference is the immediacy of published content. Historically a story could break, but may take a few hours to make TV or radio, depending on the story, now, with most people owning smart phones and using social networking sites, a story can be published within minutes of it happening, just look at the Hudson River aeroplane and the M5 crash. The first pictures and footage were from people in the midst of the story, not journalists.*

Table 14: Key Differences between Traditional PR and PR 2.0

Then	Now
• One-way top down communication. • Mainly about media relations. • Relied on traditional media to carry out your message. • Pushing messages out. • Content was mainly test (press releases) and images. • Bad news story for a company/client would hit the next day, giving PROs time to think about managing the situation and what to do to combat it.	• Two-way and encompasses feedback and dialogue. • Reaching Grunig's 'excellent' PR – two-way symmetric. • Media is richer and more distributed. • More video and linked content. • Direct communication with target audiences is possible. • Less on regional, national or international - SM is global. • 24/7 cover, instantaneous information and communication. • Greater opportunity for research.

According to Shelley Fletcher (Appendix 4, Interview 7) social media provided in a nutshell the following opportunities for PR:

- to tailor your message to your market, engage with them, build relationships and build customer and brand loyalty more effectively;
- to be timely, reactive and proactive;
- to add comment and take a local story to a national audience and platform.

Table 15: Key Advantages and Disadvantages of SM

Advantages	Disadvantages
• Communicate more effectively with both customers and the media. • Can speak directly to your audiences. • Better ability to connect and interact with stakeholders. • PR people can publish directly via social networks by e.g. creating blog platforms. • Speed and (global) reach. • Opportunities for research.	• More risk to organisations as all of their activities are potentially in public. • You cannot control social media, which in times of crisis is a massive issue. • Monitoring it is very time-consuming. • You need the skills and knowledge. • Some sectors of society or not on SM. • Fallacy that every organisation has to be doing SM.

When talking about the way social media affected the traditional Marketing Mix practitioners have somewhat different opinions, however it is clear from their perspectives below that **SM has become an integral part of the mix.**

Figure 35: Key Quotes about SM's Effect on the Marketing Mix

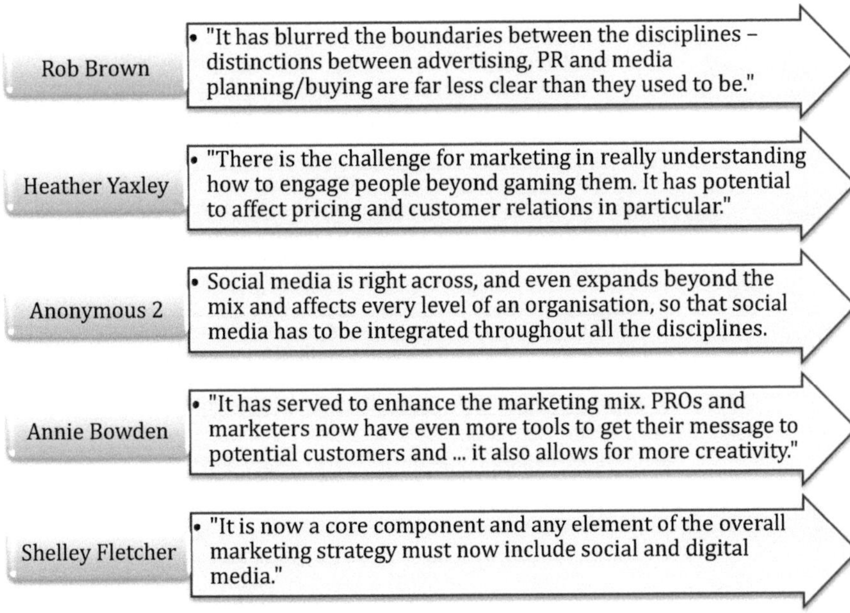

4.2.3. RQ2: Social Media Usage by PR Professionals

The questions in this section sought to identify how exactly PR practitioners use social media both in their working and private life. The following segments were categorised:

Figure 36: Main Categories for RQ2

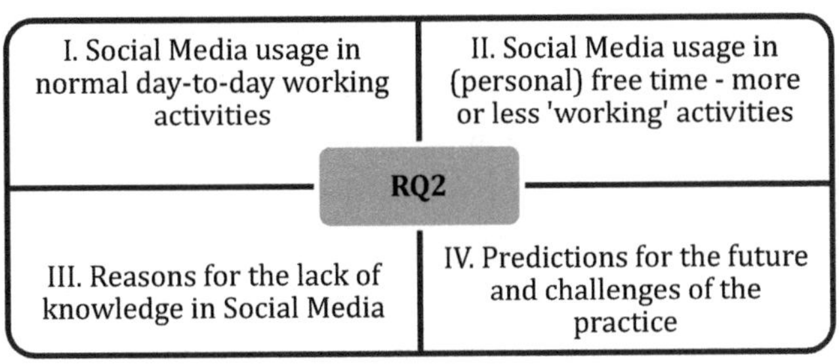

At **the office practitioners admit to be occupied by both traditional and social media**, but admittedly the latter comprises a large share of time.

Figure 37: SM Usage at Work

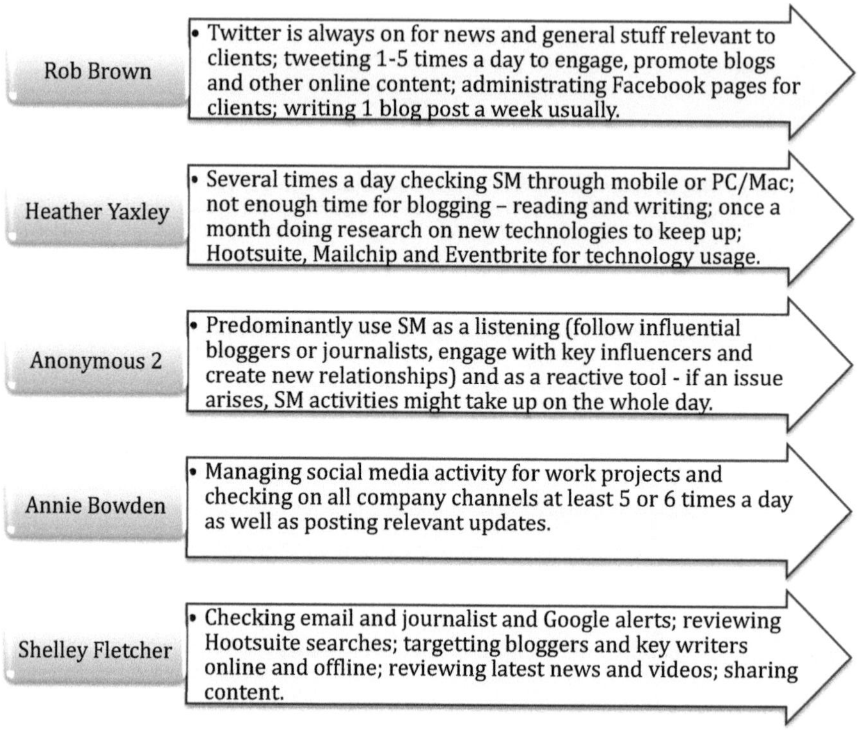

The next category aimed to find out whether practitioners nowadays spend more time 'working' (e.g. monitoring and listening in social networks) in their free time, i.e. if the emergence of SM has affected their personal lives. Practitioners admit that this issue is inevitable because **social media is 24/7 and global and not 9am till 5pm, Monday to Friday. This, in turn, makes it quite difficult to keep up or to "switch off" and is a reason for the blurring of work and private life**. Almost all interviewed 'digital immigrants' try their best to keep those separate. However, Annie Bowden, a 'digital native', admits that she does not find social media being a constant presence in her life intrusive. Shelley Fletcher argues that technology has made it much easier for her to constantly monitor SM for new opportunities for her clients even in her free time. Heather Yaxley has also noticed that thanks to new mobile technologies organisations respond to SM and emails much more out of office hours than a few years ago.

The current **lack of knowledge in social media by PR practitioners** lies according to some of the interviewees in the fact that SM is still 'new' and PROs are still learning day by day and trying their way around it to find out what works and what does not. **A challenge here is that traditional media has not gone away, so PROs need to deal with both new and old media.** Another reason is the growing importance of **multimedia and new technology, which PR practitioners tend to ignore in their preference for words.** Furthermore, because many have not grown up with SM, they are more likely to follow the 'one size fits all' strategy that naturally does not always work. Alison Theaker believes that **SM is rather a threat to many PROs because it has made it possible for everyone to communicate and by that might have decreased the need for PR services. Therefore, practitioners may believe it is not necessary to learn SM if they are going to lose their jobs anyway.**

Figure 38: Predictions for the Future of PR and its Challenges

Rob Brown

- "The PR industry needs to adapt otherwise other disciplines, SEO, advertising and digital agencies will erode the work that we do."

Heather Yaxley

- "The biggest challenge for the industry is the self-limitations of practitioners who don't see the bigger picture and will increasingly be marginalized if they don't step outside of the communications bubble to understand both the wider scope of digital/technological developments and the impact and challenges of organisations."

Anonymous 2

- Transparency and ethical implications would be the biggest challenge, especially for those who do not act accordingly, because with SM there is nowhere to hide.

Alison Theaker

- We are moving towards an age of reference where authority plays a small role and we rather trust a 'normal' person like us that we do not know but we think that they are in our situation. We are referring to other people, we are not necessarily deferring to people with authority. The more digital communication we have, the more important the human connections are.

Shelley Fletcher

- "There will always be a need for accurate and professional journalism and whether that's in print, broadcast or online, it will always be important."

4.2.4. RQ3: Measurement and Monitoring Issues

One question of the interview was concerned with the emerging issue about monitoring and measuring PR and social media activities, namely with the main challenges for doing so and suggestions of practitioners for best practices and effective ways, displayed below.

Figure 39: Issues and Challenges for Measuring and Monitoring SM

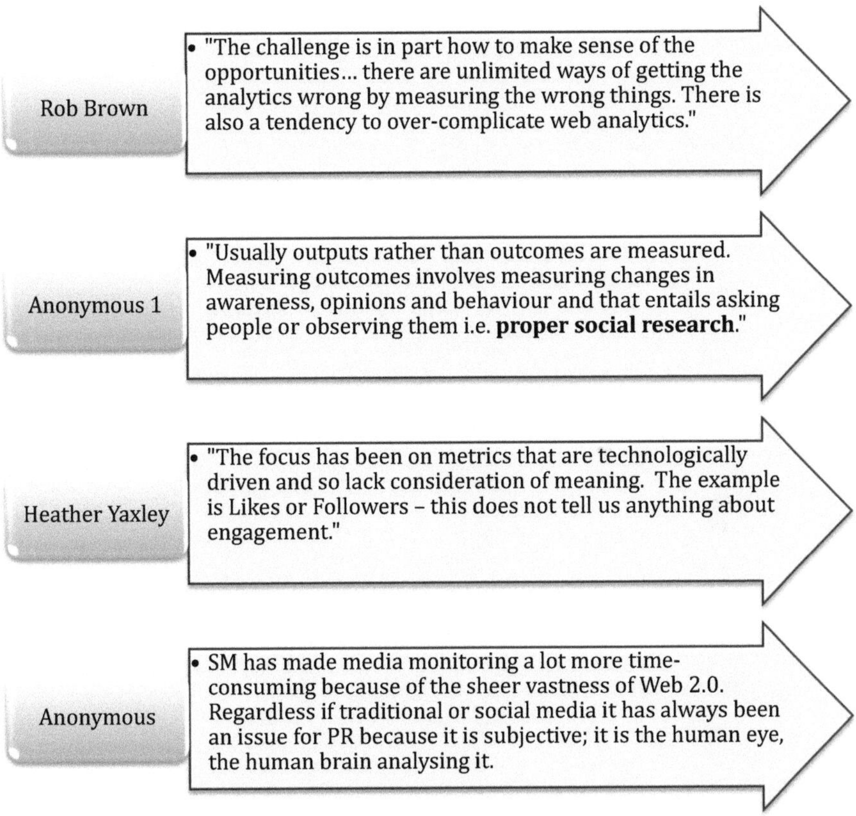

Alison Theaker furthermore says that **sales are easy to measure, engagement however is not**. Another issue, she says, is that some PROs are unwilling to learn how to use the monitoring and measuring tools that are available out there. In general, there is a **focus on quantitative, rather than qualitative measures**.

4.3. Discussion

Most findings of the secondary and primary research are in correspondence or complement each other. The literature review offered a thorough understanding on PR, social media and their integration in the Marketing Mix as well as about how SM has affected PR and how it has been used by PROs. This helped identifying the main research questions for which then the survey and interview results provided comprehensive and more detailed insights than the literature review about social media's impact on PR and especially on its usage by practitioners in both their working and private life. In summary, the findings of both the secondary and primary research indicate that social media has affected PR by being the reason for:

- Two-way conversations (dialogue) with various publics.
- More tools and channels.
- Direct, real-time, instantaneous communication.
- Better relationship-building and engagement opportunities.
- Control in the hands of ordinary people.
- Better target audience reach, locally and globally.
- Everyone can be a publisher (UGC).
- Information finds us; everything is public.
- Almost no control over what is said in SM.
- 24/7 media and demand for content.
- Everything spreads in a matter of seconds.
- Time and location do not matter.
- Crisis situations are harder to deal with.

An interesting debate arose when researching if social media has had a positive impact on PR – from the literature review it was clear that many authors believe **SM has radically changed the practice**; so do most of the interview participants. However, some of them argued that **social media has simply offered additional tools and channels, but the nature of the practice has remained the same**. They all agree though that SM has provided a number of opportunities as well as some disadvantages for the industry (described right above this paragraph) and has enhanced both internal and external communication.

As highlighted in the literature review, **the PR industry has been regarded as spin and propaganda** due to false messages being communicated. **This reputational problem is a big issue in the world of social media**, as identified from the survey and the interviews, because social media is global and public and therefore should drive transparency. However, there are still many who purposely deliver directly to publics untrue facts that have not been filtered or checked by e.g. journalists, as it was the normal case before.

In correspondence with the literature review is also the fact how interview participants agree that **social media has become an integral part of the Marketing Mix**, but it has also **blurred the boundaries between all disciplines. This to some extent endangers the future need for each of them.** Additionally however, because consumers trust people like them, not brands, advertising is much less effective, but social media, when done right, offers enormous opportunities. The fact that **PR has always been about communication and relationships, which are essential in SM, has given the practice a big advantage over the other components of the Marketing Mix**.

Both the primary and secondary research findings (European Communication Monitor and Wright and Hinson's yearly PRSA surveys) show that the usage of SM for PR has increased in the past few years. The conducted survey has offered some valuable complementary insights into this matter, namely focusing on which platforms practitioners use at the office and at home as well as for what reasons. Most of the findings were not really a surprise, as for example that Facebook is the most popular network, especially for family and friends interactions or that Twitter is mostly used for business (also mentioned by interviewees). However, **discovering that blogging is one of the least utilised ways of communication by PROs is rather shocking** and contradicts the findings of the European Communication Monitor and the survey, where blogs supposedly play an important role for communication management (illustrated in Figures 17 and 29). With regards to this, it is also interesting that only two of the interviewees mentioned blogging as a normal day-to-day working activity. Nevertheless, **the secondary and primary research show proof that SM usage has certainly**

increased, but traditional media has not been replaced, so that practitioners must take care of both.

The use of social media in their free time seems to be a very personal choice for practitioners – some have clearly separated their private and working lives, others monitor SM constantly simply because it is 24/7. **This is a very interesting issue with regards to the identified lack of knowledge and skills in social media from both the literature review and the interview results. It shows an unwillingness to learn and utilise SM in the best possible way, even after admitting that it has changed the practice to a massive extent** and that social media has been around for a few years already. As explained by one of the interviewees, this might be due to the fact that many are afraid of losing their jobs because **thanks to SM everyone can be a communicator, which in turn corresponds to the blurring of all Marketing Mix's disciplines**, where for example advertising people might do the work of PR practitioners. Nevertheless, it certainly is a challenge having to integrate both social and traditional media in the overall PR activities, but **practitioners must improve their SM knowledge and skills**, because not doing so would reflect the lower effectiveness of their campaigns as well as the engagement and interest of customers and clients. **The variety of channels has undoubtedly made it even more difficult to choose which ones are the most suitable and how to measure their effectiveness.** For example, very few have adopted using Google+ as shown in the survey results, even though it was launched last summer. Most importantly however, **PROs must learn to keep up** because the range of platforms is evolving constantly and those need to be evaluated and assessed as often as possible; campaigns must be structured and planned accordingly; every-day monitoring for new networks is necessary no matter how time-consuming it might be. **The set of PR skills and activities has without doubt become bigger and bigger with SM, e.g. SEO and blogging are/must be now essential.**

Regarding the literature review, monitoring and measuring PR has always been an issue, so has it become for social media too. Furthermore, according to the survey findings practitioners are not really monitoring the competition on SM. Nevertheless, **there are a number of tools that can be used. However, they mainly focus on the quantitative side of the matter, but lack a consideration on the subjective side, namely meanings and opinions.** The same problem has been identified by interview participants, arguing that **a proper science research is needed to actually understand the effectiveness of campaigns. Another problem is choosing the wrong tools for the wrong reasons, i.e. there is a lack of comprehensive, well-planned strategies and thereby corresponding lack of knowledge and skills.**

According to the interviewees social media plays the role of both a listening and a reactive tool and for some a platform for content creation and sharing. As many of the authors, including Brown and Solis, indicate, ordinary people have now become publishers and thereby participate and foster all conversations happening in social media. This is why companies must genuinely participate in those too, without marketing at people, but rather engaging and listening to what is being said in order to learn what customers think and want from a product or service (feedback).

Personality in social media is key to build honest relationships and win customer's trust and loyalty and by that to build a positive brand reputation. Normal people have both the influence and the power to build or destroy an image very easily and quickly through SM. Realising this should be the main reason for PROs to actually improve their SM abilities, because reputation management is a primary PR goal. As Charles Darwin once said, "it's not the strongest...that survive, nor the most intelligent but the one most responsive to change" (Say, 2010). **Therefore, in order to continue being important, the PR discipline must adapt, PROs must start learning.**

5. Conclusions and Recommendations

The research sought to thoroughly examine and describe social media's impact on the PR industry by focusing on what exactly has changed and how professionals utilise SM. The researcher believes to have **managed to find comprehensive answers to those questions, but also have identified some new problematic issues, while analysing the results, that would be a challenge for future investigations.**

5.1. Main Conclusions

As identified throughout this research, **social media has had an enormous impact on PR and has provided the practice with a number of opportunities as well as some challenges.** The overall findings of this report are:

- Social media has offered PR **new ways, channels and tools to directly communicate with various publics** by engaging in a two-way conversation, which allowed practitioners to more **easily and quickly reach target audiences both locally and globally.**
- Social media has made it **possible for ordinary people to create and share their own content and opinions publicly** on various networks and thereby **regulate the image-building of brands**. This process cannot be controlled by PROs anymore, so that they need to find new ways of participating in it.
- **Social media has been deeply integrated into all disciplines of the Marketing Mix, which has caused the blurring of those** and to some extent **endangered the need for each one**, especially for PR, since now everyone can be a communicator.
- The use of social media by practitioners has increased remarkably in the past years, however their **knowledge and skills in SM is still rather insufficient**, which for one reason is because PROs do not really use social media in their free time nor are willing to do so.
- The most utilised platforms by practitioners both at work and in private are Facebook and Twitter; blogging, however, is still not a main activity, which interestingly contradicts its stated importance by PROs.
- **Measuring and monitoring PR activities in social media is still a huge issue** that to some extent is justified by the lack of knowledge and skills in SM.

Nevertheless, there are a number of useful tools, which unfortunately mainly focus on the quantitative side, whereas PR's results are rather subjective.

5.2. Limitations

A major issue was gathering enough survey participants. The CIPR and the PRCA were asked to distribute the questionnaire to their members; however, this was not possible. Therefore, another means had to be used, as for example asking the researcher's PR connections for help to send the link to their PR contacts as well as posting the survey on various groups on LinkedIn. This is why **the sample could not have been exactly determined**, even though it was possible to monitor who was responding to the questions by checking LinkedIn users' profiles, who commented in the group discussion after filling in the survey. This all made the results less sufficient for generalisations.

Furthermore, due to financial, logistical and time issues most of the **interviews had to be conducted via email**, which nevertheless proved to be enough. However, the two face-to-face interviews provided so much additional, unplanned information, that made it possible to identify new important, but not thought of issues. Therefore, if all interviews had been in person probably a number of new issues might have arisen that would have had an impact on the study.

As always with qualitative investigations, **researcher bias** might have determined the direction of the project as well as the results analysis and interpretation. It was also very hard to choose on what to focus the most because of the vastness of the research statement.

5.3. Recommendations for Future Research

Since there are new social networks being created all the time or existing ones are improved and altered constantly, **it is essential that the impact of SM on PR is researched regularly**. Most importantly, **it would be of particular use to investigate in depth the lack of knowledge and skills and unwillingness of PROs to learn more about SM,** because it would help finding out all reasons for this problem and how professionals can solve it. Improving those abilities would certainly be a challenge for practitioners, but it has already become a necessary set of skills for the profession and for its future existence.

Also, the research focused strongly on social media. However, **it would be interesting to investigate how traditional media is being used through new media and social networks**.

Another recommendation would be to **choose different questionnaire software** than Survey Monkey, because even though it was fairly easy to use and design the questions, the free version did not allow more than 10 questions nor downloading or extracting the data so this had to be done manually and was quite timely.

As discussed above in the limitations, it is therefore recommended to **start with the primary research as early as possible**. It would be especially useful if future **researchers build good connections with influential PR practitioners**, e.g. in the CIPR, before the beginning of the research, because these people would be able to provide guidance, support and most importantly help distribute a questionnaire, since this was a big issue with this research and the researcher did not have such connections. Best thing would be to go to regional meetings of the CIPR long before the research has began and network with professionals, who could also become potential interview participants. After all, relationships in PR play a big role.

6. References

Brown, R., (2009). *Public Relations and the Social Web: How to Use Social Media and Web 2.0 in Communications.* London: Kogan Page.

Business Research, (2012). *Quantitative Research Methods: Surveys.* [online] Available at: <http://www.pbs.plymouth.ac.uk/buseres/QRMSintro.html> [Accessed 9 March 2012].

Business Research, (2012a). *Quantitative Research Methods: Experiments.* [online] Available at: <http://www.pbs.plymouth.ac.uk/buseres/QRMEintro.html> [Accessed 9 March 2012].

Butterick, K., (2011). *Introducing Public Relations.* London: SAGE Publications Ltd.

CEBR, (2005). *The Economic Significance of Public Relations.* Centre for economics and business research ltd, London. Available at: <http://www.cipr.co.uk/sites/default/files/CIPR%20full%20report%20-%20November%204%202005.pdf> [Accessed 27 October 2011].

Chaffey, D., (2009). *E-Business and E-Commerce Management.* 4th ed. Harlow: Pearson Education Limited.

CIPR, (2012). *What is PR?* [online] Available at: <http://www.cipr.co.uk/content/careers-cpd/careers-pr/what-pr> [Accessed 13 January 2012].

Collis, J. and Hussey, R. (2009). *Business research: A practical guide for undergraduate & postgraduate students.* 3rd ed. Hampshire: Palgrave Macmillan.

ComRes, (2010). *2010 CIPR: State of the PR Profession Benchmarking Survey.* ComRes, London. Available at: <http://www.cipr.co.uk/sites/default/files/CIPR%20State%20of%20the%20profession%20benchmarking%20survey%202010%20Sept.pdf> [Accessed 10 November 2011].

ComScore, (2012). *People Spent 6.7 Billion Hours on Social Networks in October.* [online] Available at: <http://www.comscoredatamine.com/2012/01/people-spent-6-7-billion-hours-on-social-networks-in-october/> [Accessed 24 February 2012].

Corporate Watch, (2003). *Public relations and lobbying industry.* [online] Available at: <http://www.corporatewatch.org/?lid=1570> [Accessed 8 November 2011].

Curiosity, (2012). *What is the impact of social media on the public relations world?* [video online] Available at: <http://curiosity.discovery.com/question/social-media-impact-on-pr> [Accessed 26 February 2012].

Davis, A., (2007). *Mastering Public Relations.* 2nd ed. New York: Palgrave Macmillan.

Daymon, C. and Holloway, I., (2002). *Qualitative Research Methods in Public Relations and Marketing Communications.* London: Routledge.

De Vaus, D., (2002). *Surveys in social research.* 5th ed. London: Routledge.

Dey, I., (1993). *Qualitative Data Analysis.* London: Routledge.

Facebook Newsroom, (2012). *Newsroom.* [online] Available at: <http://newsroom.fb.com/content/default.aspx?NewsAreaId=22> [Accessed 3 April 2012].

Fawkes, J., (2012). What is public relations? In: Theaker, A., ed. 2012. *The Public Relations Handbook.* London: Routledge. Ch. 1.

Fawkes, J., (2012a). Public relations and communications In: Theaker, A., ed. 2012. *The Public Relations Handbook.* London: Routledge. Ch. 2.

Fenton, A., (2006). *Weft QDA User's Manual.* [online] Available at: <http://www.pressure.to/qda/doc/wefthelp.pdf> [Accessed 23 March 2012].

Fielding, N., Lee, R. and Blank, G., (2008). *The SAGE Handbook of Online Research Methods.* London: SAGE Publications Ltd.

Flint, J., (2009). The Influencers are all around. *PRWeek.* September 2009. [online] Available at: <http://www.citigatedewerogerson.com/PR%20Week%20Essay%20-%20Jonathan%20Flint.pdf> [Accessed 19 January 2012].

Franklin, B., (2009). *Key Concepts in Public Relations.* London: SAGE Publications Ltd.

Gain, M., (2010). *The New PR Skills.* [online] 21 August 2010. Available at: <http://www.slideshare.net/matthewgain/working-in-a-pr-agency> [Accessed 26 February 2012].

Glide Technologies, (2007). *Journalists: How can the PR industry communicate better?* [online] Available at: <http://brandtao.files.wordpress.com/2007/08/glide_journalist_research.pdf> [Accessed 25 February 2012].

Gordon, A., (2011). *Public Relations.* Oxford: Oxford University Press.

Grunig, J. and Hunt, T, (1984). *Managing Public Relations.* London: Thompson Learning.

Guth, D. and Marsh, Ch., (2012). *Public Relations. A Values-Driven Approach.* 5th ed. Boston: Allyn & Bacon.

Healey, M.J. and Rawlinson, M.B. (1994). Interviewing techniques in business and management research. In: Wass, V.J. and Wells, P.E. (eds). *Principles and Practice in Business and Management Research.* Aldershot: Dartmouth, pp. 123-145.

Henslowe, P., (2003). *Public Relations. A practical guide to the basics.* 2nd ed. London: Kogan Page.

Hollensen, S., (2011). *Global Marketing.* 5th ed. London: Pearson Education Limited.

InfoCareIITS, (2011). *Power Of Social Media.* [video online] 30 January 2011. Available at: <http://www.youtube.com/watch?v=HOqRjNXxXBA&feature=related> [Accessed 24 February 2012].

Intersection Consulting, (2009). *Word of Mouth.* [online] Available at: <http://www.flickr.com/photos/intersectionconsulting/3406481339/> [Accessed 26 February 2012].

Kaplan, A. and Haenlein, M., (2010). Users of the world, unite! The challenges and opportunities of Social Media. *Business Horizons.* [e-journal] 53(1), pp. 59-68. Available through: Elsevier Database [Accessed 25 February 2012].

Key Note, (2007). *Public Relations Industry. Market Assessment 2007.* London: Key Note Publications Ltd.

Levine, R., Locke, C., Searls, D. and Weinberger, D., (2011). *The Cluetrain Manifesto.* 10th Anniversary ed. New York: Basic Books.

Mangold, W. G. and Faulds, D. J., (2009). Social Media: The new hybrid element of the promotion mix. *Business Horizons.* 52(4) pp. 357-365.

Mayfield, A., (2008). *What is Social Media?* [e-book] Available at: <http://www.icrossing.co.uk/fileadmin/uploads/eBooks/What_is_Social_Media_iCrossing_ebook.pdf> [Accessed 30 January 2012].

Moore, N., (2006). *How to do research. A practical guide to designing and managing research projects.* 3rd ed. London: Facet Publishing.

Phillips, D., (2009). A Grunigian View of Modern PR. *LeverWealth,* [blog] 9 January 2009. Available at: <http://leverwealth.blogspot.com/2009/01/grunigian-view-of-modern-pr.html> [Accessed 19 January 2012].

Phillips, D. and Young, P., (2009). *Online Public Relations.* London: Kogan Page Limited.

PRDaily, (2012). *The latest (and most fascinating) stats on Twitter.* [online] 24 February 2012. Available at: <http://www.prdaily.com/Main/Articles/10928.aspx> [Accessed 26 February 2012].

PRDaily, (2012a). *The most recent (and incredibly impressive) Facebook stats.* [online] 22 February 2012. Available at: <http://www.prdaily.com/Main/Articles/The_most_recent_and_incredibly_impressive_Facebook_10888.aspx> [Accessed 26 February 2012].

PRDaily, (2012b). *12 incredibly useful digital tools for PR.* [online] 4 April 2012. Available at: <http://www.prdaily.com/Main/Articles/11280.aspx> [Accessed 5 April 2012].

PRdefinition, (2011). *About The 'Public Relations Defined' Initiative.* [online] 30 October 2011. Available at: <http://prdefinition.prsa.org/index.php/2011/10/30/about-the-prsa-public-relations-defined-initiative/> [Accessed 29 February 2012].

PRSA, (2012). *What is Public Relations?* [online] Available at: <http://www.prsa.org/aboutprsa/publicrelationsdefined/> [Accessed 13 January 2012].

PRSA, (2012a). *A Modern Definition of Public Relations.* [online] Available at: <http://prdefinition.prsa.org/index.php/2012/03/01/new-definition-of-public-relations/> [Accessed 1 March 2012].

Ragan, (2012). *Consumers 71 percent more likely to buy based on social media referrals.* [online] Available at: <http://www.ragan.com/Main/Articles/44197.aspx> [Accessed 13 January 2012].

Saunders, M., Lewis, P. and Thornhill, A., (2007). *Research Methods for Business Students.* 4th ed. Harlow: Pearson Education Limited.

Saunders, M., Lewis, P. and Thornhill, A., (2009). *Research Methods for Business Students.* 5th ed. Harlow: Pearson Education Limited.

Say, M., (2010). Only the Strongest will Survive the Social Media Age. *Ecademy,* [blog] 28 July 2010. Available at: <http://www.ecademy.com/node.php?id=152919> [Accessed 7 March 2012].

Scott, D.M., (2011). *The New Rules of Marketing and PR.* New Jersey: John Wiley & Sons, Inc.

Sekaran, U. and Bougie, R., (2009). *Research Methods for Business. A Skill Building Approach.* 5th ed. Chichester: John Wiley & Sons Ltd.

Skerik, S., (2011). *Unlocking Social Media for PR.* [e-book] PR Newswire Association LLC. Available at: <http://www.prnewswire.com/knowledge-center/eBook-Unlocking-Social-Media-for-PR.html> [Accessed 21 September 2011].

Smith, PR and Zook, Ze, (2011). *Marketing Communications: integrating offline and online with social media.* 5th ed. London: Kogan Page.

Society for Human Resource Management, (2012). *An Examination of How Social Media is Embedded in Business Strategy and Operations Survey Findings.* [online] Available at: <http://www.shrm.org/research/surveyfindings/articles/pages/2anexaminationofhowsocialmediaisembeddedinbusinessstrategyandoperationssurveyfindings.aspx?homepage=mpchomepage=mpc> [Accessed 31 March 2012].

Solis, B., (2007). *PR Tips for Startups.* [e-book] Available at: <http://www.docstoc.com/docs/282060/ebook-PR-Tips-for-Startups> [Accessed 26 February 2012].

Solis, B., (2008). Introducing The Conversation Prism. *Brian Solis,* [blog] 5 August 2008. Available at: <http://www.briansolis.com/2008/08/introducing-conversation-prism/> [Accessed 25 February 2012].

Solis, B., (2011). *Engage, Revised and Updated: The Complete Guide for Brands and Businesses to Build, Cultivate, and Measure Success in the New Web.* New Jersey: John Wiley & Sons, Inc. [kindle edition].

Solis, B., (2011a). *The End of Business As Usual: Rewire the Way You Work to Succeed in the Consumer Revolution.* New Jersey: John Wiley & Sons, Inc. [kindle edition].

Solis, B., (2012). *The Rise of Digital Influence.* [online] Altimeter Group. 21 March 2008. Available at: <http://www.slideshare.net/Altimeter/the-rise-of-digital-influence> [Accessed 31 March 2012].

Solis, B. and Breakenridge, D., (2009). *PR 2.0 in a Web 2.0: What is Public Relations 2.0?* [e-book] New Jersey: FT Press.

Solis, B. and Breakenridge, D., (2009a). *Putting the Public back in Public Relations: How Social Media is reinventing the Aging Business of PR.* New Jersey: Pearson Education, Inc. [kindle edition].

Sue, V. and Ritter, L., (2012). *Conducting Online Surveys.* 2nd ed. London: SAGE Publications Ltd.

Tench, R. and Yeomans, L., (2009). *Exploring Public Relations.* 2nd ed. Harlow: Pearson Education Limited.

Theaker, A., (2012). *The Public Relations Handbook.* 4th ed. London: Routledge.

TheFutureBuzz, (2009). *Social Media, Web 2.0 And Internet Stats.* [online] 12 January 2009. Available at: <http://thefuturebuzz.com/2009/01/12/social-media-web-20-internet-numbers-stats/> [Accessed 25 February 2012].

TheRealTimeReport, (2012). *Social Media Stats: Avg. Facebook User Worth Up To $118, #RLTM Scoreboard.* [online] 3 February 2012. Available at: <http://therealtimereport.com/2012/02/03/social-media-stats-avg-facebook-user-worth-up-to-118-rltm-scoreboard/> [Accessed 24 February 2012].

Theaker, A., (2012). *The Public Relations Handbook.* 4th ed. London: Routledge.

TheTotalprofit, (2011). *The Social Media Revolution 2012.* [video online] 23 October 2011. Available at: <https://www.youtube.com/watch?v=0eUeL3n7fDs> [Accessed 24 February 2012].

Wallblog, (2011). *The future of Twitter – the Twitter News Network.* [video online] Available at: <http://wallblog.co.uk/2011/10/07/the-future-of-twitter-the-twitter-news-network/> [Accessed 12 October 2011].

Wikipedia, (2012). *Social Media.* [online] Available at: <http://en.wikipedia.org/wiki/Social_media> [Accessed 25 February 2012].

Worldometers, (2012). *Wordometers. Real time world statistics.* [online] Available at: <http://www.worldometers.info/> [Accessed 16 April 2012].

Wright, D. and Hinson, M., (2010). An Analysis of New Communications Media Use in Public Relations: Results of a Five-Year Trend Study. *Public Relations Journal,* 4(2). Public Relations Society of America. [online] Available at: <http://www.prsa.org/SearchResults/download/6D-040202/0/An_Analysis_of_New_Communications_Media_Use_in_Pub> [Accessed 21 January 2012].

Wright, D. and Hinson, M., (2011). A Three-Year Longitudinal Analysis of Social and Emerging Media Use in Public Relations Practice. *Public Relations Journal,* 5(3). Public Relations Society of America. [online] Available at: <http://www.prsa.org/Intelligence/PRJournal/Documents/2011WrightHinson.pdf> [Accessed 21 January 2012].

Yaxley, H., (2012). Digital public relations – revolution or evolution? In: Theaker, A., ed. 2012. *The Public Relations Handbook.* London: Routledge. Ch. 1.

Zerfass, A., Verhoeven, P., Tench, R., Moreno, A., & Verčič, D., (2011). *European Communication Monitor 2011.Empirical Insights into Strategic Communication in Europe. Results of an Empirical Survey in 43 Countries (Chart Version).* Brussels: EACD, EUPRERA. Available at: <www.communicationmonitor.eu> [Accessed 1 August 2011].

7. Bibliography

Bradshaw, T., 2012. Advertising sees two paths in gloom. *Financial Times.* 19 January 2012, p. 4.

Brassington, F. and Pettitt, S., 2000. *Principles of Marketing.* 2nd ed. London: Financial Times/Prentice Hall.

Bullas, J. (2012). *JeffBullas.* [blog] Available at: <http://www.jeffbullas.com/>

Burson-Marsteller, 2010. *The Global Social Media Check-up.* [online] Available at: <http://www.burson-marsteller.com/Innovation_and_insights/blogs_and_podcasts/BM_Blog/Documents/Burson-Marsteller%202010%20Global%20Social%20Media%20Check-up%20white%20paper.pdf > [Accessed 2 February 2012].

Chaffey, D., 2009. *Total E-mail Marketing.* 4th ed. Harlow: Pearson Education Limited.

CIPR social media panel, 2011. *CIPR Social Media (#ciprsm) Best Practice Guide.* May 2011 ed. [online] Available at: <http://www.cipr.co.uk/sites/default/files/CIPR_social_media%20_best%20_practice%20_guidance%20_2011_1_0.pdf> [Accessed 9 January 2012].

Curiosity, 2012. *How has the public relations industry changed over the past 20 years?* [video online] Available at: <http://curiosity.discovery.com/question/public-relations-industry-change> [Accessed 26 February 2012].

Cutlip, S.M., Center, A. H. and Broom, G.M. 2000. *Effective Public Relations.* 8th ed. Englewood Cliffs. NJ: Prentice-Hall.

Edelman Trust Barometer, 2012. *2012 Edelman Trust Barometer Executive Summary.* [online] Available at: <http://trust.edelman.com/trust-download/executive-summary/> [Accessed 25 February 2012].

Gregory, A., 2011. The state of the public relations profession in the UK. *Corporate Communications: An International Journal,* [e-journal] 16 (2), pp. 89-104 Available through: Emerald Database [Accessed 30 October 2011].

Hubspot, (2012). *Hubsport blog. Inbound Internet Marketing Blog.* [blog] Available at: <http://blog.hubspot.com/>

James, B. and Asplund, J. (2011). Making the Most of Social Media. *Gallup Management Journal,* 15 September 2011. [online] Available at: <http://gmj.gallup.com/content/149411/making-social-media.aspx> [Accessed 31 March 2012].

JeffBullas, 2011. *Turbocharging your Business with Social Media Marketing*. 13 October 2011 [online] Available at: <http://www.slideshare.net/jeffbullas/turbocharging-your-business-with-social-media-marketing> [Accessed 20 February 2012].

Journalistics, (2012). *Journalistics.* [blog] Available at: <http://blog.journalistics.com/>

Key Note, (2005). *Public Relations Industry. Market Assessment 2005*. London: Key Note Publications Ltd.

Key Note, (2006). *Public Relations Industry. Market Assessment 2006*. London: Key Note Publications Ltd.

Key Note, (2010). *Social Media Marketing. Market Assessment 2010*. London: Key Note Publications Ltd.

Key Note, (2012). *Digital Communications. Market Report 2012*. London: Key Note Publications Ltd.

Phillips, D., 2001. *Online Public Relations.* 2nd ed. London: Kogan Page.

PRBreakfastClub, (2012). *PR Breakfast Club.* [blog] Available at: <http://prbreakfastclub.com/>

PRInYourPajamas, (2012). *PR in your pajamas. Practical publicity for entrepreneurs.* [blog] Available at: <http://prinyourpajamas.com>

PRNewswire, 2011. *Nearly 60% of Business Owners Use Social Media Tools to Communicate With Their Customers.* [online] Available at: <http://www.prnewswire.com/news-releases/nearly-60-of-business-owners-use-social-media-tools-to-communicate-with-their-customers-132910543.html> [Accessed 13 October 2011].

PR-Squared, (2012). *PR-Squared. Social Media Marketing and Public Relations.* [blog] Available at: <http://www.pr-squared.com>

PRWeek, 2011. Agencies slam Wikipedia misuse. *PRWeek.* 16 December 2011, p. 3.

PRWeek, 2012. Sociability. The big picture. *PRWeek.* 17 February 2012, p. 27.

PRWeek, 2012. The FTSE 100 social media index. *PRWeek.* 10 February 2012, pp. 26-29.

Ragan, 2012. *How should we define PR?* [video online] Available at: <http://www.ragan.com/Main/Video/1573.aspx> [Accessed 13 February 2012].

Ragan, (2012). *Ragan.com. News and ideas for communicators.* [blog] Available at: <http://www.ragan.com/>

SimplyZesty, 2010. How Social Media Is Changing The PR Industry. *SimplyZesty,* [blog] 15 January 2010. Available at: <http://www.simplyzesty.com/social-media/social-media-changing-pr-industry/> [Accessed 25 February 2012].

SimplyZesty, (2012). *SimplyZesty. Online PR and Social Media.* [blog] Available at: <http://www.simplyzesty.com>

Social Media Examiner, (2012). *Social Media Examiner. Your Guide to the Social Media Jungle.* [blog] Available at: <http://www.socialmediaexaminer.com>

Social Times, (2012). *Social Times. Your Social Media Source.* [blog] Available at: <http://socialtimes.com>

Solis, B. (2012). *Brian Solis.* [blog] Available at: <http://www.briansolis.com/>

Spin Sucks, (2012). *Spin Sucks. Professional Development for PR and Marketing Pros.* [blog] Available at: <http://spinsucks.com/>

Stravellin, M., 2008. *Universal Mccann International Social Media Research Wave 3.* [online] Available at: <http://www.slideshare.net/mickstravellin/universal-mccann-international-social-media-research-wave-3> [Accessed 28 February 2012].

The Economist, (2010). *Rise of the image man.* [online] 16 December 2010. Available at: <http://www.economist.com/node/17722733?story_id=17722733> [Accessed 25 February 2012].

The Stockholm Accords, 2010. *A call to action for public relations and communication in a global society.* [online] Available at: <http://www.wprf2010.se/wp-content/uploads/2010/05/Stockholm-Accords-final-version.pdf> [Accessed 18 February 2012].

Sweetser, K. and Kelleher, T., (2011). A survey of social media use, motivation and leadership among public relations practitioners. *Public Relations Review,* 37. Available through: Elsevier Database. pp. 425-428.

Wisker, G. (2006). *The Undergraduate Research Handbook.* London: Palgrave Macmillan.

Wigley, S. and Zhang, W., (2011). A Study of PR Practitioners' Use of Social Media in Crisis Planning. *Public Relations Journal,* 5(3). Public Relations Society of America. [online] Available at: <http://www.prsa.org/Intelligence/PRJournal/Documents/2011WigleyZhang.pdf > [Accessed 5 October 2011].

Wright, D. and Hinson, M., 2008. How Blogs and Social Media Are Changing Public Relations and the Way it is Practiced. *Public Relations Journal,* 2(2). Public Relations Society of America. [online] Available at: <http://www.prsa.org/SearchResults/download/6D-

030202/0/An_Updated_Look_at_the_Impact_of_Social_Media_on_P> [Accessed 5 October 2011].

Wright, D. and Hinson, M., 2009. An Updated Look at the Impact of Social Media on Public Relations Practice. *Public Relations Journal*, 3(2). Public Relations Society of America. [online] Available at: <http://www.prsa.org/SearchResults/view/6D-020203/0/How_Blogs_and_Social_Media_are_Changing_Public_Rel > [Accessed 5 October 2011].

Wright, D. and Hinson, M., 2009. Examining How Public Relations Practitioners Actually Are Using Social Media. *Public Relations Journal*, 3(3). Public Relations Society of America. [online] Available at: <http://www.prsa.org/SearchResults/view/6D-030304/0/Examining_How_Public_Relations_Practitioners_Actua> [Accessed 5 October 2011].

Wright, D. and Hinson, M., (2010). How New Communications Media Are Being Used in Public Relations: A Longitudinal Analysis. *Public Relations Journal*, 4(3). Public Relations Society of America. [online] Available at: <http://www.prsa.org/SearchResults/view/6D-030304/0/Examining_How_Public_Relations_Practitioners_Actua> [Accessed 21 January 2012].

8. Appendices

8.1. Appendix 1: Questionnaire Design and Structure

Question 1: Has social media (including blogs) enhanced the PR practice?

○ Yes

○ No

How? (Optional)

Question 2: Which one of the following is the most important one for your organizational overall PR efforts? Please rank in priority order with 1,2,3,4 or 5 where 1 is "least important" and 5 is "most important".

	1	2	3	4	5
Blogging	○	○	○	○	○
Facebook	○	○	○	○	○
Micro-blogging (e.g. Twitter)	○	○	○	○	○
LinkedIn	○	○	○	○	○
Video sharing (e.g. YouTube)	○	○	○	○	○

If there is any other very important platform, please specify here:

Question 3: How frequently do you use each of the following in your day-to-day working activities?

	very frequently	somewhat frequently	somewhat infrequently	very infrequently	never
Blogging	○	○	○	○	○
Facebook	○	○	○	○	○
Micro-blogging (e.g. Twitter)	○	○	○	○	○
LinkedIn	○	○	○	○	○
Video sharing (e.g. YouTube)	○	○	○	○	○

Question 4: How frequently do you use each of the following in your free time?

	very frequently	somewhat frequently	somewhat infrequently	very infrequently	never
Blogging	○	○	○	○	○
Facebook	○	○	○	○	○
Micro-blogging (e.g. Twitter)	○	○	○	○	○
LinkedIn	○	○	○	○	○
Video sharing (e.g. YouTube)	○	○	○	○	○

Question 5: For what purposes do you primarily use each of the following networks?

	for social interactions with friends and family	to stay up-to-date (e.g. with trends, news etc.)	to monitor competition	to enhance business relations (e.g. with clients, journalists etc.)	to create and/or share content	I am not active there
Facebook	☐	☐	☐	☐	☐	☐
Google+	☐	☐	☐	☐	☐	☐
LinkedIn	☐	☐	☐	☐	☐	☐
Twitter	☐	☐	☐	☐	☐	☐
YouTube	☐	☐	☐	☐	☐	☐

Other purposes, please specify for the specific network:

[ ]

Question 6: Is social media less accurate and reliable than traditional media (newspapers, TV, radio etc.)?

○ Yes

○ No

Why? (Optional)

[ ]

Question 7: Are social media activities more cost-effective for organizations to develop relationships with various publics?

○ Yes

○ No

Why? (Optional)

Question 8: How long have you been working in the industry?

○ 1-3 years

○ 4-10 years

○ 10-15 years

○ 15-20 years

○ more than 20 years

Question 9: You are a PR pro, who works...?

○ in-house

○ for a major PR consultancy

○ in a boutique PR agency

○ as a freelance consultant

Question 10: What is your current occupational role?

○ Entry level position

○ Account executive

○ PR Manager/Account Manager

○ Head of Communications

○ Senior Management position

○ Director/CEO

Other (please specify)

8.2. Appendix 2: Questionnaire Results

N=80

Question 1: Has social media (including blogs) enhanced the PR practice?

98.8% (79) Yes

1.2% (1) No

How? (40 responses – all 'Yes'):

- Access to audiences and fingertip control.
- Interaction with clients, colleagues, potential customers, the general public.
- By creating a more accessible route for consumers and other businesses to connect with the source of the campaigns and provide more instant feedback.
- Another platform to communicate and influence. Speak directly to target audience.
- Opened up a whole world of communication possibilities.
- It greatly increases the channels available, provides low cost communication tools and allows targeting of diverse audiences.
- More public engagement, brand personality.
- More channels to use, faster pace. More opinions to look at as well as more competitors.
- It gives the opportunity to engage with a wider audience where traditional media can sometimes restrict reach due to the nature of their readership. Social media is far more diverse.
- Brings personality and enables consumer to speak directly to the brand.
- More exposure for client/product. Can build up relationships.
- Provided new tools that allow companies to engage their customers/prospects in a dialogue.
- Opportunity to create new channels for content (and populate these), outside traditional media. New ways to build direct links with audiences.
- It gives you a direct access to customers and audiences, it allows quick and instant messaging and once a following has been built up it is an ideal database for corporate, product and service messaging.
- A more direct form of communication with opportunities for two-way discussions. Has been beneficial for community consultation programmes.
- New ways to get directly to journalists.
- Social media is a new channel for communication with the target groups.
- Adding personal stories.
- It's made it possible to be far, far quicker in responding to (dreaded word) stakeholders as individuals and small interest groups. Such speed in response time cuts problems at the knees!
- Provides more opportunities and outlets for getting the message out.
- It has allowed us to have a better idea of how people feel about our organizations/products/issues and has given us additional avenues in which to engage with others.
- Various ways for approaching multipliers resulting in more channels for messages in a dialogue manner.
- With so many people now active on social media it would be naive to think that it had not impacted on the activities of PR professionals. The media landscape is faster moving than ever before and it is essential for PR to keep up and use social media to its advantage.
- Interaction with key audiences has been enhanced by social media. It's also great for informally getting a feel for the mood on an issue.
- By creating new, direct channels to reach targeted groups and disintermediating traditional media.
- Informing their audience of what's going on, and allowing feedback in real time.

- Any opportunity to get the "word" out undeniably has the effect of impacting reputation and visibility, both essentials in Public Relations.
- It helps us to target people that we might not be able to reach. It also helps us to develop loyalty - Facebook business pages being a perfect example.
- Now PR professionals have many more tools at hand in order to communicate whatever they want to people!
- SM is a great way to build a dialogue with stakeholders and create a corporate 'personality'. However, the momentum has to be maintained without 'flooding' the SM platforms.
- It has provided opportunities for organizations to have conversations with their audiences.
- Changed the way information is dissemintaed and in particular response time.
- PR is now not just in the papers/radio and tv but all over the web!
- Provides another means to communicate with the public and greater levels of engagement.
- Twitter is allowing us (2 x local authorities) to communicate with hard-to-reach demographics such as young people.
- More direct contact with audiences - two way.
- Speed - people and organisations look for 'instant' response; opened up the opportunity for genuine debate and for rogue or ambush marketing tactics.
- Can reach a much wider audience almost instantly. Much easier to find the information when it's no longer 'news'.
- Offered more opportunities to promote, engage and respond to issues in a public sphere.
- Transparency, 24/7, reaching new and global audiences, being able to converse directly.

Question 2: Which one of the following is the most important one for your organizational overall PR efforts? Please rank in priority order with 1,2,3,4 or 5 where 1 is "least important" and 5 is "most important".

	1	2	3	4	5	Rating Average
Blogging	18.8% (15)	17.5% (14)	28.8% (23)	18.8% (15)	16.3% (13)	2.96
Facebook	15.0% (12)	13.8% (11)	16.3% (13)	26.3% (21)	28.8% (23)	3.40
Micro-blogging (e.g. Twitter)	16.3% (13)	22.5% (18)	17.5% (14)	20.0% (16)	23.8% (19)	3.13
LinkedIn	22.5% (18)	27.5% (22)	15.0% (12)	13.8% (11)	21.3% (17)	2.84
Video sharing (e.g. YouTube)	27.5% (22)	18.8% (15)	22.5% (18)	21.3% (17)	10.0% (8)	2.68

Other very important platforms (14 responses):

- Pinterest (6)
- Online newspapers
- Foursquare
- The good old customer database and business database
- Photo sharing sites
- Company website
- Website and good old-fashioned magazine
- Quora
- Slideshare
- Email and website remain most important for us

Question 3: How frequently do you use each of the following in your day-to-day working activities?

	very frequently	somewhat frequently	somewhat infrequently	very infrequently	never
Blogging	12.5% (10)	26.3% (21)	17.5% (14)	**27.5% (22)**	16.3% (13)
Facebook	**43.8% (35)**	22.5% (18)	13.8% (11)	10.0% (8)	10.0% (8)
Micro-blogging (e.g. Twitter)	**55.0% (44)**	18.8% (15)	8.8% (7)	8.8% (7)	8.8% (7)
LinkedIn	23.8% (19)	**30.0% (24)**	18.8% (15)	18.8% (15)	8.8% (7)
Video sharing (e.g. YouTube)	7.5% (6)	**28.8% (23)**	23.8% (19)	26.3% (21)	13.8% (11)

Question 4: How frequently do you use each of the following in your free time?

	very frequently	somewhat frequently	somewhat infrequently	very infrequently	never
Blogging	15.0% (12)	21.3% (17)	15.0% (12)	23.8% (19)	**25.0% (20)**
Facebook	**62.5% (50)**	18.8% (15)	8.8% (7)	3.8% (3)	6.3% (5)
Micro-blogging (e.g. Twitter)	**45.0% (36)**	20.0% (16)	12.5% (10)	8.8% (7)	13.8% (11)
LinkedIn	22.5% (18)	**38.8% (31)**	22.5% (18)	7.5% (6)	8.8% (7)
Video sharing (e.g. YouTube)	13.8% (11)	15.0% (12)	**23.8% (19)**	**23.8% (19)**	**23.8% (19)**

Question 5: For what purposes do you primarily use each of the following networks?

	for social interactions with friends and family	to stay up-to-date (e.g. with trends, news etc.)	to monitor competition	to enhance business relations (e.g. with clients, journalists etc.)	to create and/or share content	I am not active there
Facebook	**83.8% (67)**	36.3% (29)	31.3% (25)	27.5% (22)	42.5% (34)	6.3% (5)
Google+	6.3% (5)	11.3% (9)	8.8% (7)	8.8% (7)	13.8% (11)	**70.0% (56)**
LinkedIn	5.0% (4)	38.8% (31)	21.3% (17)	**71.3% (57)**	26.3% (21)	8.8% (7)
Twitter	30.0% (24)	**62.5% (50)**	31.3% (25)	56.3% (45)	48.8% (39)	15.0% (12)
YouTube	12.5% (10)	28.8% (23)	7.5% (6)	15.0% (12)	**38.8% (31)**	31.3% (25)

Question 6: Is social media less accurate and reliable than traditional media (newspapers, TV, radio etc.)?

41.2% (33) *Yes*

58.8% (47) *No*

Why? (35 responses):

Yes

- People can put anything they want.
- Because anyone can broadcast incorrect information - there is no vetting process as there is with journalists.
- Content can be posted by anyone with any agenda.
- It's harder to evaluate the impact of social media at present, as apps like Klout are somewhat hit and miss. However, this will change in the near future.
- Regarding news, it's done `on the hoof' so less time to check facts for accuracy. Twitter is especially bad for rumours and the rumour mill to go into overload.
- Very little way to judge accuracy of reporting; presents the personal views of the blogger with no filter.
- Possibly as it's not as regulated and bloggers etc. don't always check their facts. However, journalists don't necessarily report accurately either by relying on press releases or not being balanced!
- User generated so opinionated and sometimes unverifiable.
- Because they often post unverified information.
- Social media is very accessible and its viral powers are incredible. There are now more people than ever contributing to conversations about anything and everything, meaning that there is an increased risk of incorrect information travelling far and wide. Indeed, newspapers use social networks such as Twitter as a source for stories, relying on their integrity and thus diluting the

'true' news content on occasion. Equally, it is a wonderful tool for spreading your message - whether that be personally, or as a company/news outlet - and you are able to reach so many people.

- I'm in between on this one. I think the same rule applies to both. Check the source!
- Isn't filtered by experienced editors or fact checked like most of traditional media output.
- I think it is more reliable especially when come to over throw a government and this can be seen during the events of Arab countries where we saw how people use social media to send or educate people about what was happening in those countries. This shows that social media does have a role to play but at the same time it seems that it is still struggling to do so. Platforms where people who for example open blogs for certain topics don't last long as you would compare to the traditional media and there are many journalists who follow the story by interviewing people and get to know the truth behind the events. In my own opinion I think social media sometimes is less accurate based on what was created at the first place.
- Yes & No. As with many forms of communication, some SM platforms and messages can be inaccurate - rumour, supposition - and not, necessarily, originating from the organisation involved. It can be hard, as with any rumour, to correct the perception. Having said that, it's, perhaps, no more, or less, accurate than some of the tabloids. A vague response, I know, but, for me, Yes and No.
- Depends what you mean - would Robert Peston using Twitter count as social media or traditional media? It's a false distinction, the news agenda on social media is to a degree dominated by traditional news organisations which have branched onto it as another platform.
- Not monitored, people can lie quite easily to start a TREND.

No

- Because the majority of the time they provide very succinct information. They also provide links to the original stories i.e. like Twitter or Facebook does. These are more accurate than the majority of the DAILY MAIL's articles.
- There is good and bad traditional media as well as good and bad social media. But for social media bias is expected and allowed for.
- Mostly links to online articles from traditional media.
- If anything it is more reliable as often traditional media can be very biased.
- Not a yes or no question, really. Likely to be less accurate/reliable due to speed and who's posting info (not trained journalists) but conversely likely to be more accurate because it's first-hand and direct from the individual.
- Both have their accuracy problems.
- It used to be but I think Twitter has changed everything - you still get unreliable and fake reports, but they occur in traditional media too (increasingly even as staff numbers shrink). I get most of my news via Twitter now and find it very rare that it is wrong/incorrect/false, whereas our local paper often (at least twice a week) contains major inaccuracies in its reports. The balance has shifted in the past 2 years.
- It's just quicker; so you have to be available to respond.
- Social media is breaking news as fast as traditional outlets now.
- It can be because traditional media still tend to want verification before running news stories; however, it doesn't have to be less accurate and reliable. Sometimes, first-person experience is very real and compelling.
- People post honestly about their opinions - journalists are more easily influenced.
- You have a lot of the credible news outlets releasing breaking news on social media. However there is a greater likelihood releasing wrong non-credible news due to their rush of wanting to break the story first.
- It certainly has the ability to "go viral" without sources being standardized or necessarily checked, but the "Wikipedia effect" where false information gets weeded out as it picks up visibility does

the job of removing falsities from a story. One should nonetheless always remain critical.

- Social media are as much reliable and accurate as traditional media at the moment. Whoever intends to create publicity is able to do it either ways.
- Messaging is different and often not 'filtered' so it can be both more and less representative.
- It depends on what the source is and whether it is trusted. There is probably more scope for inaccuracy in social media but this can often be identified.
- They are each available to the public via a filter. With traditional media that is the editorial/ commercial parameters of the media and its owners; in social media it is the preferences and opinions of the uploader and the responders.
- Not if you know the more reliable sites and people to check. It can be more up to date and with more details.
- All depends - cannot say that one or the other is more or less accurate and reliable.

Question 7: Are social media activities more cost-effective for organizations to develop relationships with various publics?

77.5% (62) *Yes*

22.5% (18) *No*

Why? (29 responses):

Yes

- It depends on which aspect of the public you are targeting. If you are doing PR for wind farms, the majority of the target audience is 50+ as they are more inclined to dislike the project and are also not as adept as younger generations when it comes to social networking. If you are doing PR for a music festival however, social networking is the best free advertising you can get.
- Creative use of social media can create more leverage at a lower cost because it is cutting edge and free.
- Can be used during desk time of staff and on mobiles while travelling but there is a human resource cost to be factored in, i.e. it's not free!
- Publics come to you, though time/cost is a factor.
- Maybe, maybe not. People perceive that social media is less expensive but they also tend to do it off the cuff without putting the time and effort into developing messaging or to really learn how to use the platforms. I see too many companies who hire interns to run their SM programs because they know how to blog, or Tweet, but who have no strategic understanding of how to influence an audience or communicate a message.
- They can be but organisations should never be fooled into thinking they're free - they always require time and resource, and time costs money, whether it's in-house or an agency cost. Done well, and for the right organisation, social media can be very cost effective - it all depends on what's right for the organisation.
- Our comms budget has been frozen due to government cuts, so social media has been an important channel as we have the in-house expertise to use and monitor it effectively.
- Yes, if done right, no if done wrong.
- Because your message reaches a larger target group.
- Can reach people one-on-one and one-to-many with the same tools. It's low cost; however, one's key audiences must have access to it and use it as well for it to be cost effective.
- Because you have to interact and must not only spread messages.
- I think whether you answer yes or no to this question largely depends on the industry in which you work. For me, as I work within the third sector and do not actively seek clients for example, it is fantastic. I am able to easily engage with a huge variety of people/organisations for free through our Facebook and Twitter channels as well as to a lesser degree with YouTube, Flickr and

Pinterest accounts. We do not need to spend money on more traditional marketing and utlise our social media networks very effectively to both publicise our acitivies as well as build relationships with our stakeholders/the public. However, other businesses may need to rely more heavily on more traditional routes of relationship building to flourish and may place less emphasis on social media.

- It really depends on the goals companies originally have for social media, and how they measure its effectiveness. It can take a lot of time and effort - and once you start, you cannot stop!
- Social media takes the place somewhat of "traditional" platforms such as advertising, but spreading the word (word of mouth, status sharing, going 'viral') these are all opportunities to gain awareness while circumventing traditional marketing strategies and promotion.
- Because a Social Media the PR Professional has to do a lot of search in order to allocate the public he wants to develop relationships with.
- They can be as one-to-one relationships can be developed more quickly which filter across the platform. SM is, at least for the moment (!), free so, as long as the communications are valid, it can be more cost-effective.
- Yes for some but not all. It reaches a wider audience in terms of reach figures. But not all segments of publics.
- They're cheap to use although the volumes of data involved can be time consuming.

No

- It depends on the level of activity you want to participate in, e.g some social media campaigns can lead to big expenditure, and also the development of the campaigns may take in traditional and non traditional media.
- Not yet because we still do both. That might change.
- People forget that time is money, so it's not a cheap communications tool.
- Social media is becoming as important as other mediums and with that comes cost to do it right.
- They can be - but only if done properly and effectively. This might take some training - and I certainly wouldn't let a client of mine launch into it on their own.
- It depends on the organization and the publics - it can be very cost effective for B2C, often less so for B2B and it can be very resource intensive if you are going to do it effectively.
- Qualified personnel cost what they cost, no matter what type of work they are engaged in. The primary cost of well done social media is the pay check.
- They still take human resource for developing content, monitoring and responding.
- It takes a lot of time and there are still relatively few people using them - our main demographic doesn't.
- Actually, probably yes but as yet this impact has not been properly tested and quantified.
- Takes time to do well and time costs money.

Question 8: How long have you been working in the industry?

38.8% (31)	1-3 years
26.2% (21)	4-10 years
10.0% (8)	10-15 years
11.2% (9)	15-20 years
13.8% (11)	more than 20 years

Question 9: You are a PR pro, who works...?

47.5% (38)	in-house
15.0% (12)	for a major PR consultancy
17.5% (14)	in a boutique PR agency
20.0% (16)	as a freelance consultant

Question 10: What is your current occupational role?

22.5% (18)	Entry level position
13.8% (11)	Account Executive
21.2% (17)	PR Manager/Account Manager
3.8% (3)	Head of Communications
10.0% (8)	Senior Management position
16.2% (13)	Director/CEO
12,5% (10)	Other
Some specifications for 'Other'	• Editor & Co-owner of a newspaper • Communications Consultant • PR & Communications Officer • Press Fleet and Events officer • PR & Marketing Research Professional • Communications Assistant • University Lecturer, Educator or Professor

8.3. Appendix 3: Interview Design and Structure

Interview questions

(Dissertation on "The Impact of Social Media on the PR Industry")

1. How do you think the emergence of social media changed PR? Is it a positive or a negative impact and why?

2. What are the main differences between traditional PR and PR 2.0?

3. What opportunities does social media provide? What are the advantages and disadvantages?

4. How do you think the emergence of social media affected the Marketing Mix?

5. What are the main challenges of measuring PR and social media activities? What do you think is the most effective way of measuring them?

6. Can you please briefly describe a normal working day? What are your usual day-to-day activities; how much of them are combined with social media, e.g. how much time of your workday do you spend in blogs and social media networks etc?

7. Does this change affect your personal life? Do you spend relatively more time "working", e.g. monitoring social media and networking, in your free time now in comparison to let's say 6 years ago?

8. What are your predictions for the future of the practice and what do you think would be the biggest challenges for the industry?

Do you prefer your name and personal data to remain confidential?

- [ ] Yes
- [ ] No

Would it be OK if I post the interview on my blog (www.iliyanastareva.com); of course I would say (and link) who you are, what you do, how to contact you etc?

- [ ] Yes
- [ ] No

Thank you!

8.4. Appendix 4: Interview Transcripts

Interview 1:

Interview participant:	Rob Brown
Occupational role:	Managing Director of Rule 5
Years in the industry:	ca. 20
Educational background:	Economics and Politics (BA)
Additional:	Author of 'PR and the Social Web: How to use Social Media and Web 2.0 in Communications', intensively referenced in the literature review
Date of interview:	7 February 2012
Type of interview:	Email due to geographical distance and time constraints

9. How do you think the emergence of social media changed PR? Is it a positive or a negative impact and why?

It has changed PR considerably. A core element of traditional PR has been media relations. The media has evolved and so must PR. From a structural point of view there is more dialogue and more peer to peer communication and PR must engage with and learn to influence these conversations. From a practical point of view media is generally richer and more distributed. In the past our content was mainly test (press releases) and images. No we need to consider including more video and linked content. PR people are even learning to share HTML code.

10. What are the main differences between traditional PR and PR 2.0?

I've answered partly above but that main difference is that PR historically was one-way top down communication. Now it has to be more two-way and encompass feedback and dialogue. PR is less about control and more about discussion. This means that strategically PR people are advising clients on best practice rather than how to spin communications to give an impression of best practise. I think we need to drop the term PR 2.0. This is mainstream PR as it is now.

11. What opportunities does social media provide? What are the advantages and disadvantages?

One major advantage is that PR people can publish directly via social networks of by creating blog platforms. Many enlightened PR people have built big social media communities that enable them to do this more effectively. A disadvantage if you can call it that is that there is more risk to organizations as all of their activities are potentially in public.

12. How do you think the emergence of social media affected the Marketing Mix?

It has blurred the boundaries between the disciplines – distinctions between advertising, PR and media planning/buying are far less clear than they used to be. Social Media also allows communications tasks to be achieved in new ways.

13. What are the main challenges of measuring PR and social media activities? What do you think is the most effective way of measuring them?

The challenge is in part how to make sense of the opportunities. The web is infinitely measurable, but that also means there are unlimited ways of getting the analytics wrong by measuring the wrong things. There is also a tendency to over-complicate web analytics. Basic measure like site visits, twitter followers, retweet numbers, Facebook likes can also be useful but they are measure of quantity rather than quality and therefore have limitations. Measuring outcomes is far more powerful. Can the analytics tell us how in terms of behaviour, action or views and opinions the campaign met the set objectives?

14. Can you please briefly describe a normal working day? What are your usual day-to-day activities; how much of them are combined with social media, e.g. how much time of your workday do you spend in blogs and social media networks etc?

No such thing as an average day. Twitter is always on and glanced at regularly for general news and stuff that is relevant to clients. I'll posts tweets usually 1-5 times a day mainly to keep engaged with the community by sharing opinions and links. I also use my social media communities (client/agency/personal) to promote links to blog posts and online content. I'm an admin on two client Facebook pages so I will look at those most days though the content is managed by colleagues. Most weeks I'll draft a blog post. Most days I'll read several although if the site is trusted I don't really distinguish between blogs/mainstream media.

15. Does this change affect your personal life? Do you spend relatively more time "working", e.g. monitoring social media and networking, in your free time now in comparison to let's say 6 years ago?

Yes, absolutely. It can be really difficult to switch off.

16. What are your predictions for the future of the practice and what do you think would be the biggest challenges for the industry?

The PR industry needs to adapt otherwise other disciplines, SEO, advertising and digital agencies will erode the work that we do.

<u>Interview 2:</u>

Interview participant:	Anonymous 1
Occupational role:	Confidential
Years in the industry:	ca. 20 (both professional and academic)
Educational background:	Confidential
Additional:	Internationally recognised academic researcher; has written and edited a number of books as well as a number of journal articles about PR
Date of interview:	12 February 2012
Type of interview:	Short email due to geographical distance and time constraints

1. How do you think the emergence of social media changed PR? Is it a positive or a negative impact and why?

I want to tackle your question in a slightly different way. Social media has changed the way organisations interact with their stakeholders in terms of the range of stakeholders they now engage with, the shift in power because of the ability of those stakeholders to hold them to account very publicly and to all parts of the world at any time. PR, as the functional discipline responsible for maintaining and building those relationships with stakeholders has to change too in order to rise to the challenge and opportunities this brings for organisations. PR has to be competent in the use of SM channels and content, but it also has a major advisory role to enable senior managers to understand how SM works, why they can't ignore it and what new obligations it lays on them. Of course SM means all the usual things like having cover 24/7, having access to people in the organisation who can answer questions, having quick clearance routines for potentially controversial content etc.

It is positive in that it provides new, disintermediated channels for organisations that can interact in personal ways with whole groups of people it either never knew or had pretty distant relations with, or who were always close, but now can be even closer. It is negative because of the accountabilities I mentioned which can be demanding and unforgiving if you ever make a mistake.

2. **What are the main challenges of measuring PR and social media activities? What do you think is the most effective way of measuring them?**

Usually outputs rather than outcomes are measured and for example Google Analytics is about outputs or reach. Measuring outcomes involves measuring changes in awareness, opinions and behaviour and that entails asking people or observing them i.e. proper social research. There is no escape from that and it is always the best way.

Interview 3:

Interview participant:	Heather Yaxley
Occupational role:	Part-time lecturer at Bournemouth University Educator of the CIPR qualifications Managing Consultant at Applause Consultancy (Self-employed) General Secretary at Motor Industry Public Affairs Association
Years in the industry:	ca. 15-20 (professional and academic)
Educational background:	Psychology (BA) Currently doing a PhD in Career Studies in Public Relations
Additional:	Author of two chapters in 'The Public Relations Handbook', intensively references in the literature review, and others.
Date of interview:	22 February 2012
Type of interview:	Email due to geographical distance and time constraints

1. **How do you think the emergence of social media changed PR? Is it a positive or a negative impact and why?**

It has given a new focus to tactical skills primarily in terms of the perspective that younger practitioners are best equipped to undertake social media. I don't believe social media have fundamentally changed PR – although they have increased immediacy, global reach and the need to engage (and build relationships) directly rather than just through intermediaries. I think it is positive, but also has negative sides especially if PR is restricting itself by viewing its domain as Twitter, focusing primarily on campaigns, outsourcing to agencies or not developing a strategic approach.

2. **What are the main differences between traditional PR and PR 2.0?**

As above, I see it mainly in functional terms as speed and reach since the basic skills of understanding communications, relationship building and managing reputation are largely unchanged. It also offers great opportunity for research – although this needs to be balanced by recognition that not all sectors of society are engaged or participating in SM.

The real potential of PR 2.0 – is probably PR 3.0 – where aspects such as the semantic web and convergence of various ways of accessing information will escalate further. The future also is multimedia which in recent years PR practitioners have tended to ignore in preference for thinking in words only.

3. **What opportunities does social media provide? What are the advantages and disadvantages?**

As above. Disadvantages are also that the focus is on something seen as "new and shiny" and so the facts that many sections of society are not digitally engaged (and don't wish to be) may blind practitioners to the need to not automatically think of an SM initiative. I also think that belief that young people prefer this medium is overblown.

4. **How do you think the emergence of social media affected the Marketing Mix?**

As with PR there's been primarily focus on marketing communications at a tactical level through SM – particularly Facebook. There is the challenge for marketing in really understanding how to engage people beyond gaming them (likes on Facebook tied into competitions etc). It has potential to affect pricing and customer relations in particular, although the responsiveness of organizations is lagging behind what could be done. Obviously online purchasing has been a challenge to many brick-based retail organizations – but again there needs to remain a balance as not everyone can and will shop or research/seek information online.

5. **What are the main challenges of measuring PR and social media activities? What do you think is the most effective way of measuring them?**

The focus has been on metrics that are technologically driven and so lack consideration of meaning. The example is Likes or Followers – this doesn't tell us anything about engagement. Likewise cumulative measures of Followers is meaningless. There needs to be more engagement with qualitative measures and also looking beyond the 'size' aspects of data for data's sake.

6. **Can you please briefly describe a normal working day? What are your usual day-to-day activities; how much of them are combined with social media, e.g. how much time of your workday do you spend in blogs and social media networks etc?**

It varies depending on what else I have going on, but using mobile devices (Blackberry, iPhone and iPad) as well as PC/Mac to check SM is easy and I do this probably a few times a day. Blogging is something I'd like to do more in terms of reading and writing, but time is a consideration for me here. Getting to grips with new technologies becomes a real challenge – but I probably try once a month at least to undertake research to keep ahead of what is going on. I've found services such as Eventbrite, Mailchimp and Hootsuite are great in terms of how they enable you to use technology to save time and money, whilst tapping into digital and social aspects of communications.

7. **Does this change affect your personal life? Do you spend relatively more time "working", e.g. monitoring social media and networking, in your free time now in comparison to let's say 6 years ago?**

I'm self-employed so have viewed work as 24:7 pretty much over last 12 years. What I have noticed is that increasingly those in companies using mobile technologies respond to SM and email much more out of hours than say 2-3 years ago.

8. What are your predictions for the future of the practice and what do you think would be the biggest challenges for the industry?

I think that PR needs to upscale from responding to all technologies in a tactical, new toy way. There will be more integration and PR practitioners are in danger of being one trick ponies (we know how to write...) and so losing out on the more strategic overview position that SM needs. The biggest challenge for the industry is the self-limitations of practitioners who don't see the bigger picture and will increasingly be marginalized if they don't step outside of the communications bubble to understand both the wider scope of digital/technological developments and the impact and challenges of organizations.

<u>Interview 4:</u>

Interview participant:	Anonymous 2
Occupational role:	Press and PR Manager (in-house)
Years in the industry:	ca. 7
Educational background:	Journalisms
Additional:	Prefers to stay confidential
Date of interview:	24 February 2012
Type of interview:	Face-to-face; 45 minutes (below is a response summary)

1. How do you think the emergence of social media changed PR? Is it a positive or a negative impact and why?

First of all, it has changed PR to an absolutely massive extent. I look back at what the industry looked like when I joined it and I think that if somebody had said to me 7 years ago what it was going to be today I probably wouldn't have believed them. Mostly social media is a very positive thing; I think it's made the industry be a lot more transparent which obviously is very, very important for the ethics. At the moment the PR industry is becoming self-regulated and that can and has had in past issues in terms of ethics. I'm a big believer in transparent PR and a dialogue, which means listening, which is a hugely important part, as well as getting your message out there and social media has really, really helped do that. With social media there is nowhere to hide, so I'd say positive means from getting your message out there and you no longer have to rely on traditional media to carry your message for you; you can talk directly, I'd say directly 'with' rather than 'to' your audiences and you can get their feedback on any number of things and that would also help you start shaping your behaviour as an organisation. That feedback and listening that you didn't have before is much quicker, that's the beauty of social media, it's instantaneous, it doesn't matter what your geographical location is, what time of day or night it is. So, social media has opened a huge amount of channels for us, it has introduced a lot of new audiences that we would not have been able to engage with before; it has enabled PR professionals to 'go global' in terms of reach and influence. But obviously there is a flip side to that as well and I'd say probably the biggest one is reputation – if something doesn't go well it will spread wildly and fast on social media and you cannot control social media, so it will be a lot more difficult to manage issues and crisis situations because you have to react much more quickly. There really is nowhere to hide! Everything is public now! But from a personal perspective, the downside of social media is that it has replaced face-to-face communication a little bit. Nevertheless it's a great communication tool especially for large organisation and even in the case of employees communicating to each other; let's say if the CEO has to say something to everyone in the company, social media is a great way of doing it and also for employees to engage with the organisation itself and learn about what's going on.

2. What are the main differences between traditional PR and PR 2.0?

Obviously with social media you don't rely on someone else to carry your message, you can speak directly to or with your target audiences and you can listen to them; it's a lot faster and instantaneous; it's much further reaching; it's 24/7. There isn't much of an emphasis anymore on regional, national or international because social media is global. Therefore, you can reach a specific audience on a global network much easier and this is a huge opportunity in terms of talking to new audiences.

3. What opportunities does social media provide? What are the advantages and disadvantages?

In a nutshell: advantages would be the global reach, the fact that it is instantaneous, the fact that you can speak directly to your audiences. The disadvantages would be when it comes to crisis or issues management you cannot control social media and monitoring it is very time-consuming.

4. How do you think the emergence of social media affected the Marketing Mix?

Well, what I would say there has always been a bit of a debate between marketing and PR; there has always been a sort of a conflict – who does what, who's responsible for what; is marketing more important etc. I personally think if it is a more of a communications case, then PR would come first and marketing will support this; if it is more of a business issue, then marketing would come first and PR will support this – it's reciprocal. And social media is right across, and even expands beyond the mix and affects every level of an organisation, so that social media has to be integrated throughout all the disciplines.

5. What are the main challenges of measuring PR and social media activities? What do you think is the most effective way of measuring them?

Everything is public now. Social media has made media monitoring a lot more time-consuming because of the sheer vastness of Web 2.0 especially if you are representing a large and well-known organisation with potentially tens of thousands of interested stakeholders. Also a few years ago you would've been looking at the newspapers and listening to the radio, but now you've got all these other channels as well and you cannot ignore them, they are highly influential. So we actually use media monitoring software where we'll get what we call the world cuttings through each day compared to the old days where you cut the articles from a newspaper. So we have a press department that takes care of broadcast media, social media, print media, basically taking care of all the coverage monitoring and analysis for probably two hours a day. There are also a number of companies out there completely dedicated to monitoring and analyzing social media and when you think about the fact that this is the only purpose of those companies (and it is a lucrative business) it shows how highly influential and far reaching social media is. Among other things they can provide access to conversations, identification of key influencers, measurement of the above key metrics and conducting comparisons between competitors and topics. In the end, measuring and monitoring, regardless if traditional or social media it has always been an issue for the PR industry because it is subjective; it is the human eye, the human brain analysing it. One might think something is positive, someone else would say it's negative or neutral. There has always been a large amount of measurement tools, say for example some measure the column inches to represent the influence, but the PR industry has never only appealed to one single tool. And again, social media is another complication here. So, there are lots of different ways of measurement depending on what the issue is or the desired outcome, however in general this would include monitoring/analysing:

- Social media traffic in terms of tone, demographic, geography etc.
- Trends
- 'Likes'
- Translation (eg. subsequent website hits, a rise in sales, attendees signing up for an event etc.).

6. Can you please briefly describe a normal working day? What are your usual day-to-day activities; how much of them are combined with social media, e.g. how much time of your workday do you spend in blogs and social media networks etc?

In our department we predominantly use social media as a listening and of course as a reactive tool to help us with our environmental scanning. So listening for us means to follow influential bloggers or journalists and thereby we try to engage with key influencers and create new relationships. And of course we monitor our own networks and what is being said about our organisation, regardless of it being negative or positive, and we try to engage with those people and come into a dialogue. I personally, spend a lot less time in social media because I am responsible on the strategic and management level. Of course, if an issue arise on social media it could take us the whole day; and everyone will be on it, including me. But it every much depends on what's happening during the day. So social media is just a part of all, a smaller part, but I think that if you ask me the same question in a few years, the years will be very different.

7. Does this change affect your personal life? Do you spend relatively more time "working", e.g. monitoring social media and networking, in your free time now in comparison to let's say 6 years ago?

Yes, but this is inevitable as social media is global and 24/7. It does not operate 9-5! Personally, I am not on social media; I have no profiles on social media! I use it rather as a listening tool, for example I do have an account on Twitter, but I don't tweet, I only follow people and monitor what they are tweeting. I prefer to keep my professional and personal life separate and try my best. Admittedly though it is inevitable for those to blur.

8. Do you think there is a lack of knowledge and skills in social media among PR practitioners? What are the reasons for this?

Oh Absolutely, I agree. First, because it is very new and second, because it is always changing, so it is very hard to keep up. But I don't think anybody really saw this coming in terms of the extent of its importance and impact, so I'm more than happy to admit that we are still learning day by day. People are still searching and feeling the way and looking at what's working and what doesn't. And it's not like traditional media has gone away, this is on top of it, it is much more encompassing, so it is more like we are following social media, rather than social media is following the industry. What matters is that you should not underestimate it and you have to learn from your mistakes and continue trying to get better at it. Right at the beginning when social media emerged many just jumped in the bandwagon with two feet and said "Oh, we have to do this" and got it wrong because you have to first ask yourself the question "Do I need to do social media, why and how to use it correctly?" You need to look at who you want to reach, what you are trying to achieve, what your objectives are. Social media is not always the best choice.

9. What are your predictions for the future of the practice and what do you think would be the biggest challenges for the industry?

Social media has had positive ethical implications for the PR industry in terms of supporting and furthering two way dialogue and transparency and I feel this will continue to be the case as it is the only way to operate successfully in this new digital era – this is probably also one of the biggest challenges as for those who do not act ethically, with social media there is nowhere to hide! But, I really can't answer that question! If someone once told me about social media and the situation now I wouldn't have believed it. Anything is possible! Anything can happen!

Interview 5:

Interview participant:	Alison Theaker
Occupational role:	CEO at The Spark (freelance consultant)
Years in the industry:	ca. 30 (professional and academic)
Educational background:	Journalism
Additional:	Author of 'The Public Relations Handbook' (a principal PR textbook since the 2000s), intensively references in the literature review.
Date of interview:	8 March 2012
Type of interview:	Face-to-face, 40 minutes (below is a response summary)

1. **How do you think the emergence of social media changed PR? Is it a positive or a negative impact and why?**

I think the emergence of social media doesn't change the nature of what PR is at all; rather it has offered new channels and tools.

I agree with Paul Holmes that for good PR people digital changes nothing. So if you were doing good PR 10 years ago, if you were having conversations with people if you were being open and honest and responsive to people, social media is just a new channel. But first you need to define your objectives. It is ridiculous to say that everyone has to tweet or whatever; you need to know why you are doing it and who you are talking too. A lot of people I think are just doing it in a broadcast way, so not really using it according to the actual idea of social media; and you have this tension, it is SOCIAL media, but you are using it for a BUSINESS purpose. A lot of people just promote and talk about their product but others won't follow them or listen to them.

People running businesses are responding to this awkward feeling "Oh my God, I ought to be doing this, I should be doing this, I don't have enough time to do it, oh I'm scared of it, oh I don't believe in it", then they may say "nothing's happened" or "it's fantastic." But they still haven't really thought about what their objectives are for engaging with social media, or how they could be interesting to the people they meet there. If you talk too much about your business, people won't follow you and you've got to be interesting and you've got to be generous, and follow the rules of etiquette. A lot of people out there are not following them however. And if you are a PR practitioner representing a company you have to follow these rules. Many aren't, for example Edelman's 'flog' for Walmart, when a couple was supposedly going around the country and blogging about their experience, but actually they were just two Edelman's employees doing it in their office – that's not just damaging the client there, but also the image of PR.

But if you go back to Grunig's excellence theory, it is a great tool because it gives you the ability to talk directly to your publics, you don't have to go through the media, you have a direct connection, you can engage and you can respond. So theoretically – fantastic! Actually, it's not happening enough. So I don't think it changes the nature of PR, it's just that people are using that tool and are making some 'excellent' PR.

2. What are the disadvantages and advantages of social media?

In the latest Zerfass European Monitor research, a lot of PR people said that they thought social media was a threat. Many are scared, because if anyone can do social media, why pay for PR. So they think, "If anyone can communicate now, why would they need us?" But they need to realise that it is useful if you use it well and in the right way. It is not instant, though. People who are good at it now, have been doing it for at least two years. Just putting your name out there, let's say on Facebook, is just advertising, not PR. If the people that you need to talk to are digital natives, it's great. But if the people that you need to communicate with are digital immigrants, the older generations, they are less engaged, so you need to have other methods as well.

3. What are the main challenges of measuring PR and social media activities? What do you think is the most effective way of measuring them?

Measurement has always been a big issue, although it is getting better. If you are using Google Analytics or Adwords, you can easily see how many people come to your site and where they have found it, or if they came to it through Facebook, Twitter etc. All the necessary tools for measurement and analysis are out there, but I have rarely come across a PR agency that is really good at it. Engagement is harder to measure; sales we can measure. So it's important to take note of where engagement comes from. The best PR practitioners plan their objectives and decide on the methods of how to measure them – the tools are there. Gut feeling doesn't work! More people need to learn how to use the available tools.

4. How is the industry going to solve this problem?

I don't think it's going to happen; it's not going to solve it. This will continue. And this reflects the reputation of the industry – for example some are changing the name to communications management etc. This 'licensing' however doesn't work. So, we want to call ourselves PR professionals, but if you look at other professions, this is nothing like them. If you get a group of PR people in one room they are never going to agree.

5. Does this change affect your personal life? Do you spend relatively more time "working", e.g. monitoring social media and networking, in your free time now in comparison to let's say 6 years ago?

Oh no, it hasn't changed for me; I've always been good at separating my personal and professional life. I'm working for myself and the whole point of it is not having to work seven days a week, so whilst I am online most of the time in my working week, I am not on social media longer than I need to be.

6. Do you think there is a lack of knowledge and skills in social media among PR practitioners? What are the reasons for this?

Many people just go out there and say "oh look I've got 15,000 followers!" but what matters is how you translate this into influence. Many business owners just don't know WHY they are on social media. And they think it will solve all of their problems but it doesn't. As always, what works best is a combination of methods and you have to know why you are adding it into that combination.

7. What are your predictions for the future of the practice and what do you think would be the biggest challenges for the industry?

In all four editions of The Public Relations Handbook since 2001 I have had a chapter on the future of PR. What's really interesting is what's changed and what's stayed the same. We still have reputation issues, we still are going on about measurement and people have finally 'woken up' to globalisation. New technology is always a challenge, because there are always new things coming along and you have to learn to use those tools correctly. A single tool is never going to be the only answer. I think what's really interesting is that, as Kevin Murray has said, we are now in an age of reference where authority plays a smaller role and we are more likely to trust a 'normal' person like us.

We are referring to other people, we are not necessarily deferring to people with authority. And I believe this is what we will have to deal with. It's not like at the time of Ivy Lee when you could send your press release and people thought "Oh well, that's reasonable then." People now are "No, no, we don't believe you" and they are less likely to believe a big company now. The more digital communication we have, the more important the human connections are. In social media you have got to have a personality and communicate in a different way. And in another 10 years, we'll still be talking about reputation, I'm sure.

Interview 6:

Interview participant:	Annie Bowden
Occupational role:	PR & Communications Officer at the **Royal Society of Wildlife Trusts**
Years in the industry:	ca. 5
Educational background:	Journalism (PgDip) Geography (BA)
Additional:	Digital native
Date of interview:	12 March 2012
Type of interview:	Email due to geographical distance and time constraints

1. How do you think the emergence of social media changed PR? Is it a positive or a negative impact and why?

I think social media has forced PRs to sit up and take notice of the digital world and the impact of its activities within it. The PR industry now has to be even more reactive than ever before – before services like a bad news story for your company/client would hit the next day, giving you time to think about managing the situation and what you were going to do to combat it. Now, a story can be both live and viral within minutes, cutting down the time in which you are able to manage the crisis. This can, of course, be a good thing too and something that PRs can use to their advantage if they are savvy in their use of social media tools, particularly Twitter. Being a child of the digital age, I think the increasingly use of social media is a great thing and is something that we can use to our advantage in terms of communicating with stakeholders and spreading good news. There are definitely more challenges presented by its emergence but I think the PR industry should embrace social media and utilise it strategically and creatively rather than fear its existence.

2. What are the main differences between traditional PR and PR 2.0?

I think the key difference is probably the pace at which things move. In a world of newspapers, radio and television you have an awful lot more time on the ball, so to speak, and have the ability to plan in a more structured fashion and spend less time being reactive as a consequence. In the digital world, things move very fast. A story can be online within seconds and that can work both to your advantage and present you with challenges if things aren't going quite how you hoped! We are also able to reach a much wider audience more easily now than ever before, which is great.

3. What opportunities does social media provide? What are the advantages and disadvantages?

The effectiveness of social media for your business really depends on what it is that you do. For example, in my career I have worked for a professional sports team, a college and a charity, for all of whom social media is a fantastic tool. I have been able to interact with fans, students and stakeholders with a casual ease that you can't necessarily foster through some more traditional methods. I can contact people with our messages at any time of day or night from anywhere and really build a relationship with them and I think that personal touch is a wonderful side effect of social media – though it can very quickly take over your life! At RSWT (Royal Society of Wildlife Trusts), we are able to utilise a number of different social media platforms (Facebook, Twitter, Pinterest, Flickr and YouTube) as what we do is so varied and I am able to provide each of those channels with relevant content and resultantly people interact with it. However, a lot of businesses are making the 'one size fits all' mistake with social media and signing up to each and every platform because it's what they think they should be doing rather than taking the time to consider what would work for them and their business and put their efforts into that rather than trying to manage a number of unsuitable efforts. As I have discussed above, social media can also be an absolute nightmare if you are on the wrong end of a conversation. It's great to spread a positive message quickly, but a negative one will spread even faster making it challenging to cope with!

4. How do you think the emergence of social media affected the Marketing Mix?

I think it has served to enhance the marketing mix. PROs and marketers now have even more tools at their disposal to get their message to potential customers and that is definitely a good thing, in my opinion. I think it also allows for more creativity in marketing, which again is exciting.

5. What are the main challenges of measuring PR and social media activities? What do you think is the most effective way of measuring them?

The key issue is of course proving its worth. Unlike traditional marketing, it is very difficult to prove that your social media activity has an actual conversion rate into customers, it's hard to prove ROI which has always been what managers look to as a measure of effectiveness. I personally use a number of tools, such as Klout and the in-built Facebook insights, to measure how effective our social media activity is in terms of engagement. For me, the aim is to get more and more stakeholders engaging with us through our social activity and increase followers/likes to increase the reach of our content. We are slightly different in that we are not attempting to attract customers, so engagement is key.

6. Can you please briefly describe a normal working day? What are your usual day-to-day activities; how much of them are combined with social media, e.g. how much time of your workday do you spend in blogs and social media networks etc?

As I work over two projects (Biffaward and Local Food), my time is usually divided fairly evenly between them. Both require traditional PR support in terms of writing and sending press releases, approving releases from projects, dealing with enquiries from projects and/or media outlets, updating websites and so on. I also manage the social media activity for both projects and check on all our channels at least 5 or 6 times a day as well as posting relevant updates too. This is linked intrinsically with all the press activity we engage in as we are keen to spread the coverage through these channels as part of our content. I am also responsible for the organisation of an annual awards ceremony for one of the projects, which is taking up a fair chunk of my time at the moment.

7. **Does this change affect your personal life? Do you spend relatively more time "working", e.g. monitoring social media and networking, in your free time now in comparison to let's say 6 years ago?**

As a child of the social media age, I've always got my iPhone to hand to check my personal social media channels, which are linked to my work ones too. Personally, I don't find it intrusive as I really enjoy the social media side of my job but it is definitely a constant presence!

8. **Do you think there is a lack of knowledge and skills in social media among PR practitioners? What are the reasons for this?**

I think that is probably fair, but social media is still fairly new to a lot of people. I am young and have been brought up using a computer and smart phones so I don't struggle with the use of social media. But some of my older colleagues who have not been surrounded by social media do struggle a little more with it. We are, as an industry, still discovering what works and what doesn't so it would be naive to assume that we knew all the answers and were doing everything as well as we could as I am sure there are many more interesting theories and tactics to come!

9. **What are your predictions for the future of the practice and what do you think would be the biggest challenges for the industry?**

I think social media will continue to lie within the PR and marketing mix but I don't think it will be to the detriment of – or will even replace – more traditional marketing methods. It will become just another tool that we use to help spread a message, something that is second nature.

Interview 7:

Interview participant:	Shelley Fletcher
Occupational role:	Strategic PR & Marketing Consultant and Business Owner at Firegrass Communications
Years in the industry:	ca. 5-10
Educational background:	Social Sciences (Certificate) Marketing (Professional Certificate by the CIM) Business Studies (Certificate)
Additional:	Devon & Cornwall Regional Co-ordinator and Committee Member at the CIPR - **West of England**
Date of interview:	17 March 2012
Type of interview:	Email due to geographical distance and time constraints

1. How do you think the emergence of social media changed PR? Is it a positive or a negative impact and why?

It is both positive and negative; it provides opportunities to reach and engage with a broader market and communicate more effectively with both your customers and the media, however, the availability of social media channels means that everyone can now be a publisher, editor and journalist.

On the one hand this is good as it give control to individuals to share content, however it also means that not everything you read has been effectively researched and stories / blogs etc are no longer always impartial. It also means that there are now more inaccuracies – think back to playing Chinese Whispers, no matter how hard you try, it is very difficult to ensure a message remains 100% accurate when it is passed though many people and channels.

As PR professionals we have to adapt our behavior and approach to make the most of the new media channels and find ways to manage our clients' messages and reputations online as well as in the traditional media. In my opinion both have to work hand in hand and a good PR strategy must include online and traditional PR tactics.

2. What are the main differences between traditional PR and PR 2.0?

We used to talk at people, tell our stories the way we wanted them to be told and effectively just push our messages out. In the emerging world of PR 2.0 it is now about communication, engagement and listening. Our messages and the way in which we communicate our messages have now changed and we now need to look more closely at how our customers wish to receive messages, this could be by reading stories in a magazine or newspaper, or it could be online through Facebook and other social networking platforms.

Once a story is published online it now presents an opportunity and forum for debate. Content can be easily shared, promoted further, but it can also create a platform for debate from the public and other interested parties, something that needs to be monitored by PRs.

The main difference is the immediacy of published content. Historically a story could break, but may take a few hours to make TV or radio, depending on the story, now, with most people owning smart phones and using social networking sites, a story can be published within minutes of it happening, just look at the Hudson River aeroplane and the M5 crash. The first pictures and footage were from people in the midst of the story, not journalists.

3. **What opportunities does social media provide? What are the advantages and disadvantages?**

It provided the opportunity to tailor your message to your market, engage with them, build relationship and build customer and brand loyalty more effectively.

It provides the opportunity to be timely, reactive and proactive.

It provides opportunity to add comment and take a local story to a national audience and platform.

As with most things, the clue is in the name – 'social' networking – it's all about being social and engaging, not just trying to sell products and services.

It does require monitoring and effective management. It is not an opportunity for staff to spend all day on Facebook – it needs to be managed strategically, just the same as if you were deciding where to place advertising and monitoring conversion rates of campaigns and specific activity.

4. **How do you think the emergence of social media affected the Marketing Mix?**

It is now a core component and any element of the overall marketing strategy must now include social and digital media. In my opinion, no company can successfully market themselves without adopting some online tactics, be that ecommerce, social networking, blogging and targeting online media and bloggers. Of course it depends on the products, services and customers, but I do not believe that any business can ignore the opportunities the online PR presents.

5. **What are the main challenges of measuring PR and social media activities? What do you think is the most effective way of measuring them?**

I believe that everything needs to be measured against agreed objectives; this may be increased website hits from social sites, use of an offer code or increased brand awareness. But ultimately, any activity should be measured in terms of increased profits. If the activity is working, and the objective is increased sales, then sales should increase.

It is difficult to measure value in terms of AVE / EVE, but personally I do not believe AVE and EVE are a fair reflection or measurement tactic. Having worked client side myself, the value of editorial in terms of what an advert would have cost me does not help me increase my bottom line, but increased sales will. All PR activity, not just social media, should, in my opinion be designed to increase sales and therefore be measured accordingly.

6. **Can you please briefly describe a normal working day? What are your usual day-to-day activities; how much of them are combined with social media, e.g. how much time of your workday do you spend in blogs and social media networks etc?**

- Checking email
- Checking journalist alerts in emails
- Reviewing Hootsuite searches for key search terms that relate to clients
- Targeting bloggers and freelance writers, exactly as I would with print and broadcast targets
- Reviewing the local daily paper and weekly papers

- Checking Google alerts that have been set up for all clients and key phrases
- Reviewing latest breaking news and industry stories to identify opportunities for client comments
- Reviewing latest audio and visual content to identify opportunities for clients
- Sharing relevant content online
- Issuing media release to target journos (traditional and digital)
- Engaging directly with key journos either via email, phone or Twitter
- Checking #journorequests for any opportunities

7. Does this change affect your personal life? Do you spend relatively more time "working", e.g. monitoring social media and networking, in your free time now in comparison to let's say 6 years ago?

I do monitor social media, the news and emails a lot, but the only difference today to say six years ago, is that there are more platforms to monitor. I have always been aware of news and potential opportunities for my clients, whether that be 11am on a Monday morning or 3pm on a Sunday afternoon, that's my job.

Technology now has actually made this easier; I now have alerts and key searches set up which mean I can more easily 'cut through the noise' and react quickly to opportunities. I am always looking for opportunities for my clients and, as we live in a time of 24 hour news, opportunities don't always happen Monday to Friday, 9 to 5!

8. What are your predictions for the future of the practice and what do you think would be the biggest challenges for the industry?

Very difficult to say. Social will continue to be important, but I don't believe that traditional will cease. There will always be a need for accurate and professional journalism and whether that's in print, broadcast or online, it will always be important. I am sure more social sites will emerge and I predict that PR will have to become even more targeted for specific mediums and with tailored messages.

I think we will find even more ways to engage with our customers and publics and may even find companies and products being developed as a direct result of customer engagement, consultation and demand.